HOW TO BE A SUCCESSFUL SECONDARY TEACHER

Also available in the series

How to be a Successful Secondary Teacher

Sue Leach

continuum
LONDON • NEW YORK

Continuum International Publishing Group

The Tower Building	80 Maiden Lane
11 York Road	Suite 704
London	New York
SE1 7NX	NY 10038

www.continuumbooks.com

British Library Cataloguing-in-Publication Data
A catalogue record for this book is available from the British Library.

ISBN: 0-8264-8517-0 (paperback)

Library of Congress Cataloging-in-Publication Data
A catalog record for this book is available from the Library of Congress.

Typeset by Ben Cracknell Studios
Printed and bound in Great Britain by MPG Books Ltd, Bodmin, Cornwall

Contents

Introduction

'The only good teaching is that which outpaces development.'

(Lev Vygotsky (1962), *Thought and Language*, Cambridge, MA: MIT Press)

THE ORGANIZATION OF THIS BOOK

This book aims to take you through some of the key thinking, preparation and evaluation processes necessary for successful teaching. Chapters are organized in a roughly chronological way to cover important concerns to be borne in mind before you teach a lesson, while you teach a lesson, and after you have taught a lesson. As you become more proficient and confident you will begin to see the indivisibility of the whole undertaking, in the sense that everything you do is contingent on everything else you do.

Each chapter is followed by a summary of the recommendations made within it for thinking, consideration and action, and by the standards for the Award of Qualified Teacher Status implicitly referred to. Appendices cover: pedagogy, the requirements of the National Curriculum across subject areas, how to improve pupils' handwriting, and information about the Teacher Effectiveness Enhancement Programme.

WHAT THIS BOOK COVERS

The book seeks to develop your thinking and understanding, and to help you develop a holistic view of teaching and learning. It is not aimed at teaching in any one subject area, though much of what is suggested relates to teaching in classrooms or laboratories rather than in gyms or on sports fields. The book is not a 'tips for teachers' text. Instead, it is aimed much more at encouraging you to reflect in an informed way on your teaching, and to use this reflection to formulate theories on which to base further teaching, and to inform reading and research. While much of what is said here will help you consider issues implicit in the Standards for the Award of Qualified Teacher status, the book as a whole is not explicitly focused on these standards, and therefore does not offer advice, for example, about the pastoral responsibilities of teachers, nor about working as a member of a whole school staff.

The book begins by focusing on pupils, rather than on you as a teacher, or on any other aspect of education. As pupils are the whole reason for the existence of the education system in the first place, an informed, thoughtful understanding of pupils, of their learning and of yourself in relation to pupils, is central to the whole undertaking of teaching. It is reasonable to assume that you are aiming to be a secondary teacher because you feel some kind of commitment to young people, or at least to teaching in general, and wish to contribute as positively as you can to pupils' educational experiences during the period of statutory schooling between 11 and 16, and possibly afterwards. It will be implicitly assumed throughout the rest of this book that you have such a commitment; what follows is consciously shaped to place pupils and their learning at the centre of all your endeavours, and to encourage you to develop an informed understanding of how to work collaboratively and progressively with them during your career.

REFLECTION AS AN ONGOING FEATURE OF YOUR DEVELOPMENT

Developing your ability to reflect on your daily experiences, and to arrive at a deeper understanding of how and why lessons worked out as they did, and why pupils behaved as they did, is a key part of your developing expertise as a teacher. This reflection, as a consciously analytical, self-aware and self-critical undertaking, does not come naturally or easily to everyone, and often needs to be worked at in a very deliberate way. The reflection needed in relation to learning to be a teacher, and continuing throughout your career as a teacher, depends crucially on several things:

- your ability to place yourself in the position of the pupils as receivers of your lessons;
- your ability to see your lesson from a perspective other than your own;
- your ability to analyse the teaching/pedagogical implications of your lessons.

So, for example, if you thought you had planned a really good lesson, and the teacher you were working with had thought it would work well, but the lesson did not go at all as planned, you are left wondering what went wrong. At this stage it is important that you acquire the reflective skills that will help you resolve such problems, in addition to listening to the advice of experienced teachers. A good way of developing your reflective skills is to keep a daily journal or diary. On some Initial Teacher Training (ITT) courses this is an expected part of the course. You should use this to revisit your experiences of the day, and to consider how to learn from them. The quiet and private consideration of what has happened to you during the day, based on a real intention to learn about yourself from it as well as learning about your pupils, will prove very beneficial in the course of your training year.

YOUR READING, RESEARCH AND TRAINING

During your training to be a teacher, you will have been exposed to a wide range of information, opinion and expertise designed to develop your overall grasp of this huge undertaking called 'teaching'. Some of this range will have included perspectives based on research findings; much of the reading you have done and that has been recommended to you will have been concerned with classroom-based research. A significant and increasingly important source of school-based research is that published by the National Strategy, and by the Qualifications and Curriculum Authority (QCA). Much of this is worth reading carefully as it shows in very accessible (if often overly detailed) ways how key understandings about pupils and learning can be brought to bear on lesson planning and classroom teaching. Most of this particular research has been carried out according to tight specifications laid down by the particular funding body; it is often therefore research which is seeking to confirm a theoretical position already decided upon, or to underpin specific practical classroom approaches that are deemed desirable.

Other reading will undoubtedly have been based on research seeking to open up lines of enquiry relating to wider issues than those covered in the kind of research described above. This reading is possibly more useful in helping you develop an understanding of the importance of continuing to be a learner throughout your career. This wider, more academic research, like all other research, inevitably has its own implicit agenda, but this should not deter you from continuing to read it in order to develop your thinking.

You are encouraged to take every opportunity to extend your expertise and understanding by continuing to read and research; essentially, to ensure that you engage in your continuing professional development, and recognize that your continued learning is central to your success.

WHAT IS A SUCCESSFUL TEACHER?

As this book aims to help you become a successful secondary teacher, it might be useful to consider what could be taken to mean 'successful' in this context. There is a range of possible interpretations. A successful secondary teacher is probably one who:

- is organized, prepared and in control at all times;
- understands the centrality of continuing reflection and research in order to improve teaching and learning;
- understands the pedagogical rationale underpinning successful teaching;

- teaches lessons which pupils find challenging, and which consciously contribute to pupils' development;
- manages pupils positively and professionally in order that lessons are well run, purposeful and focused on pupils' learning;
- enables pupils to perform well, or above predictions, in tests and examinations;
- in subjects other than core subjects, recruits above-average numbers of pupils for GCSE courses;
- recruits above-average numbers of pupils into post-16 study, in 11–18 schools.

All or any of these definitions can be applicable at different times, and to different teachers. You are encouraged to use this list to inform your development towards this level of professionalism.

Chapter 1

Attitudes and approaches to pupils

This chapter aims to help you use your personal experiences of schooling to reflect on pupils in schools now, and to consider your present understanding of pupils in relation to your development as a teacher during your training year and afterwards.

YOUR ATTITUDES AND APPROACHES TO PUPILS

Your attitudes and approaches to pupils are fundamental to becoming a successful secondary teacher. This may appear to be so obvious that it does not need saying. However, as you might have learned from your own experience, not all the teachers you encountered during your school days shared this view. It is therefore important that you spend time thinking about how to develop your relationships with and understanding of pupils. You might like to bear in mind that pupils are required by law to be educated, though not necessarily in school, and that the overwhelming majority of them are taught within the formal education system. Within that system, failure to attend, for whatever reason, is increasingly monitored and controlled, sometimes resulting in the imprisonment of parents for not ensuring the daily attendance of their children. In contrast, you are becoming a teacher because this is a profession you have chosen. The implications of this potentially fundamental contradiction of interests and motivation are worth considering; you can do nothing to alter this situation, but you can take account of it in your daily interactions with your pupils.

You undoubtedly already have views about pupils, and you may have taken the opportunity to gain experience of pupils by working in schools before you commenced your training. At this stage, therefore, you need to be conscious of the many preconceptions which you are inevitably bringing to bear on your training, and above all on your approaches to pupils. You are encouraged to look carefully and thoughtfully at these and to consider the range of perspectives given below which will contribute to your developing expertise in the classroom.

Teachers who demonstrate 'best practice' in their work:

- recognize their responsibility for the learning of **every** pupil in their classes;
- know that subscribing to ability labelling and ability-related practices is likely to be detrimental to pupils' learning[1] and attempt to work against school-based norms, therefore:
  - recognize their role in promoting a positive learning environment in which all pupils are valued and acknowledged;
  - understand how to work with pupils in the most positive ways;
  - know how to support pupils' learning fairly and rigorously.

It will take time to reach this level of expertise, in addition to all the other areas in which you will need to develop, and it is therefore suggested that you look closely at the following in order to establish a baseline from which to start. Before you proceed, consider whether you understand the bullet points above, and the extent to which you do or do not agree with them. It will also be useful for you to note any queries you have about them, which further sections in this book will help you with.

YOUR PAST EXPERIENCE OF EDUCATION

It is useful to think back to your own experience as a pupil in school in relation to your current training. Many of your expectations, attitudes and intentions will inevitably have been shaped by this past experience, and it is possible that your very intention to become a teacher relates back to your educational past. With regard to pupils, it is worth considering to what extent your attitudes towards such things as pupils' motivation and willingness to be taught, pupils' needs and pupils' behaviour have been influenced by your experience. In addition, it is useful to reflect on the examples of teacher/pupil interaction which you observed or experienced during your education, and to evaluate the extent to which these have remained with you as models either of what to do, or what not to do.

Think about your own schooling

You may not retain very clear memories of your time as a pupil, but it is still worth attempting to reconstruct the educational experiences you have had from your point of view as a pupil. School experiences for many people can have a powerfully negative effect on their later lives, if only at the regrettable level of alienating them from the system entirely. This in turn affects the way in which they shape their children's view of schooling, and can lead to very real problems of communication between the school and its client parents. It can be assumed that your experiences have on the whole been positive ones. However, it is worth spending time on the following exercise in order to help you relive the emotional impact that your varied experiences had on you. Like most people, you probably have vivid memories of how you were made to feel by negative and unfair treatment you received from teachers, and it is worth remembering your responses. In discussion with your peers you will find that the ways in which you responded and still respond are not unique.

Consider your memories of primary education:

- What do you remember of the experiences at school which shaped your behaviour and attitudes? Can you remember any adaptations you had to make in order to fit in?
- What were the positive aspects of your primary schooling?
- What were the negative aspects?

- Were you conscious of being part of some kind of hierarchy of achievement?
- What attitudes did your teachers have towards you?
- In what ways did your teachers differentiate in their treatment of and attitude towards pupils in your class?
- Were you ever hurt or upset by the ways in which teachers treated you?
- What was it that upset you?
- Has this affected your attitude towards any of your educational experiences since then?
- What do you remember of the expectations you took with you when you started at your secondary school?

Consider your memories of secondary education:

- What happened to your expectations at secondary school?
- How were year groups organized for teaching purposes? Sets? Mixed ability? Banding? Where were you placed within this structure? How did you feel about this?
- What do you remember about the behaviour, attitudes and achievement levels of your peers who were regarded as 'high, middle or low ability'?
- If you were labelled as anything other than 'high ability' in some subject areas, how did this make you feel about yourself as a learner?
- What do remember of the attitudes towards pupils which your teachers displayed in their teaching? What are your opinions about these now?
- What made some teachers and their lessons more attractive to you than others?
- What memories do you still carry with you of times when you were hurt or upset by the way teachers treated you?
- What do you feel most influenced your attitude to different teachers and the subjects they taught?

If you remember your passage through schooling as marked by more success than failure and positive rather than negative treatment by teachers, you are likely to regard the education system in a positive light. You are also likely to find it difficult to understand the perceptions of people who have had a less positive educational career than you. However, as you wish to become a teacher, you are encouraged to take a probing look at the perceptions of teaching and education that you acquired during your schooling from the point of view of being a pupil, and attempt to apply this understanding to situations you encounter during your teaching career.

YOUR EXPERIENCE OF YOUNG PEOPLE

You will probably also bring with you into your training year some experiences of young people which you may have acquired through relationships with siblings or other relatives, through working with young people in organizations including educational establishments, through private tuition, or through some other undertaking. Again, it is worth your while to consider the extent to which these experiences have shaped your attitudes about teaching, pupils and schools.

PREVIOUS ACQUISITION OF INTERPERSONAL SKILLS/TRAINING

You may be fortunate in having learned some of the current theory and practice of so-called interpersonal skills. This will stand you in very good stead in your teaching, and will help you establish productive and learning-oriented classroom practices and approaches. The overall aims of interpersonal skills are to maximize the positive aspects of relationships within working environments, and in the case of teachers, to enable them to establish the best learning environment possible for their daily work.

You may have acquired some of these skills already, through working in a range of occupations, particularly those involving members of the public, or possibly through drama work of some kind. In all cases, the emphasis is on:

- knowing how to be a good listener;
- being able to maintain appropriate eye contact;

- knowing a vocabulary likely to promote understanding and to avoid confrontation;
- knowing the importance of body language;
- knowing how to defuse situations, through the application of many of these skills;
- knowing how to use your voice appropriately, including deliberate use of tone, pitch and volume;
- knowing how to avoid provoking aggression, by not pushing people into corners from which they cannot escape without loss of dignity;
- recognizing the validity of other points of view;
- resisting the temptation to dominate other people, or to show that you 'know best'.

If you have not come across these skills so far, it would be sensible to find out more about them. In your training you are not necessarily going to be explicitly taught about all these skills, though undoubtedly they will all be touched upon. Obviously, many of these skills have a direct bearing on overall class management, an area which will be covered in a later chapter.

UNDERSTANDING PUPILS FROM OTHER PERSPECTIVES

It is important that you develop an understanding of what affects pupils' performance and behaviour in the classroom, and in school generally, and that you continue through your career to refine and modify this understanding. It is therefore also important that you recognize the centrality of *learning* in your approach to working with your pupils, and some attention paid at a more theoretical level to the psychology of learning will be of advantage as you continue to develop your teacher identity. This is particularly useful in reflecting on those pupils who appear to be 'lazy'. The quite common practice on the part of teachers of talking about pupils as lazy is a shorthand way of saying a great many things about pupils, which may not be much to do with actual laziness. There are any number of reasons why pupils do not do what teachers want them to do at the time teachers want them to do it. The list includes:

- genuine tiredness, which may be self-induced through staying up far too late, or because a pupil has to take major responsibilities at home as a carer or substitute parent, or for undiagnosed medical reasons;
- no energy due to lack of adequate nutrition, usually affecting pupils who have had no proper breakfast;
- lack of understanding of the task, disguised as something else in order not to lose face;
- inability to see properly – many pupils have sight problems which remain untreated;
- inability to hear properly – again, pupils have hearing problems which are not always adequately treated;
- lack of motivation, separate from any of the above, itself caused by any number of factors;
- the genuine effect of puberty on adolescents, producing all sorts of feelings of alienation, self-doubt, uncertainties about relationships, family problems.

As you will discover later in this book, there are many ways in which to motivate and remotivate pupils, in spite of all the conditions listed above. Your challenge is to acquire the skills to do this.

YOUR EMOTIONAL RESPONSES

Teaching is a very personal, and therefore emotionally involving, undertaking, which can face you with aspects of yourself in a way which you might find very challenging. You are encouraged to consider your emotional make-up, and your understanding of how it might affect your classroom performance and your relationships with pupils. It is often the case, for example, that where trainees still lack a range of strategies for working effectively with young people they may find their emotions becoming the dominant factor in their reactions rather than a more sophisticated, emotionally neutral professional approach. Your reactions are likely to follow similar patterns to those you have already learned during your life so far, and it is therefore important that you develop a clear understanding of how you are likely to feel in the kinds of situations which regularly occur in classrooms. This recognition will then need to be consciously worked on, in order that you can use it productively to shape and control your professional persona in the classroom.

Some examples are offered here of the kind of situation which can call up inappropriate emotional responses from you, and which you should learn to manage where necessary over the course of this training year. You need also to recognize that when pupils sense that they have affected a teacher emotionally (got them 'on the run', made them cry, made them lose their temper), they can quickly get the better of that teacher, and will continue to try to use similar tactics in each lesson until something happens to change their behaviour.

- pupils barely pay you any attention as you enter the room/attempt to get the lesson under way;
- pupils do not respond to any of your questions;
- pupils continually call out;
- pupils continue to hold private conversations;
- pupils don't listen to your explanations;
- pupils react aggressively to your reprimands;
- pupils refuse to move seats when you ask them to do so;
- pupils challenge you over disciplinary statements you have made;
- pupils refuse to take you or your lesson seriously;
- pupils claim that they have already done the work.

You will undoubtedly come across other instances of pupil behaviour which initially unbalance you and momentarily make you lose belief in what you are doing. Possible emotional responses on your part to these examples of inappropriate behaviour are:

- anger or irritation;
- negative self-consciousness;
- frustration;
- rapid loss of confidence;
- helplessness;
- strongly authoritarian stance with a determination to impose your control;

- panic;
- crying.

During your training year you will learn a range of ways of pre-empting inappropriate behaviour from your pupils. You will also, hopefully, learn how to manage your emotional responses, in order that you can remain confident and consistent in the classroom. A good start is to go through the first list and consider which, if any, of the reactions in the second list you are likely to feel in response. It is also a good idea to consider which of these examples of undesirable pupil behaviour could be pre-empted by class management strategies and the use of approaches to learning which quickly engage pupils in the lesson and make misbehaviour redundant, and which allow you to remain emotionally neutral. There is ample evidence to suggest that teachers who remain calm, consistent, firm and fair enjoy greater success and sense of achievement in their teaching than teachers who do not. Obviously, there is much more to the successful running of a classroom than this, but these behaviours do need to be part of your general repertoire of teaching strategies.

SUMMARY

This chapter aimed to give you some useful points for reflection about yourself in relation to pupils.

- consider your preconceptions about pupils, teaching and schools;
- consider your memories of primary and secondary schooling;
- construct a pupil's perspective of education;
- consider your overall attitudes to young people;
- develop your understanding of what affects pupils' behaviour and performance in classrooms;
- consider how you might react emotionally in a range of classroom situations.

STANDARDS

This chapter will help you consider some of the issues implicit in the following standards. Trainees:

1.2;   treat pupils consistently, with respect and consideration, and are concerned for their development as learners;

3.3.1;   have high expectations of pupils and build successful relationships, centred on teaching and learning. They establish a purposeful learning environment where diversity is valued and where pupils feel secure and confident.

NOTE

1 For more information see Hart, S. *et al.* (2004), *Learning Without Limits*. Maidenhead: Open University Press. This excellent book challenges received notions of ability, making clear the highly damaging effects they have on children, and suggests other ways of thinking about children and their development.

Chapter 2

Expectations of pupils

This chapter builds on Chapter 1 and aims to develop your thinking about pupils from the perspective of expectations. Some sections in this chapter offer further amplification of key points made in Chapter 1. It is possible that you already have ideas about what you will expect of your pupils, both with regard to their behaviour and with regard to their learning. This chapter will support you in further developing your ideas and understanding.

To start with, it is worth considering what is meant by expectations, and what are the factors which shape teachers' and pupils' expectations about themselves and their performance. From the teacher's perspective, expectations are largely shaped by:

- past familiarity with pupils and their performance;
- an internalized, generalized idea about what can be expected of pupils according to their age and 'ability';
- test and examination grades of new pupils;
- the sets pupils have been placed in;
- what other teachers say about pupils;
- information conveyed formally about pupils;
- first impressions of pupils, on which teachers sometimes build predictions about performance five years into the future.

Expectations tend to be about the following:

- how pupils will respond to particular content, teaching approaches and classroom organization;
- how individual pupils will respond and behave in a variety of situations;
- a concept of what pupils' finished work might look like;
- an understanding of where extra help and explanation might be needed to further understanding;
- a clear belief about what can and cannot be undertaken with any particular class of pupils.

The factors which shape pupils' expectations of themselves are discussed later in the chapter.

EFFECT OF WHAT TEACHERS SAY ON YOUR EXPECTATIONS

The opinions of other teachers about pupils can have a powerful effect on the ways in which you think about the pupils in your classes. The sharing of views about pupils which can occur in staffrooms, often at the level of gossip and often conducted in negative terms, is quite a seductive situation for the trainee teacher, or the newly qualified teacher; if you are involved in it, it has the effect of confirming your status as a member of staff, and it can act as a way of affirming your relationships with your colleagues. On the other hand, sharing of views and experiences of pupils can be done in a very positive and useful way, though this is more likely to occur within the context of positively focused departmental meetings; it is sensible to be aware of what kind of talk about pupils you are being invited to contribute to. At this stage of your career it is a good idea to try to remain uninfluenced by what others say about pupils, and instead to keep an open mind, and to look upon all your pupils as learners with unlimited potential.

Teachers' low expectations can give rise to situations where you are working alongside a colleague who considers a lesson you have planned to be too difficult for the pupils. You may have nevertheless gone ahead and taught the lesson anyway, and may have found that the pupils were quite able to achieve what you aimed for. In such a case, the teacher may have acknowledged their mistake, and used the whole experience as the basis for a discussion about the effect of expectations on pupils' performance; on the other hand, the teacher may have decided that this was a one-off, and dismissed it. In either case, what occurred was an interesting exemplification of expectations in practice, and you are encouraged to use this as an experiential base on which to build a more sophisticated understanding of expectations and how they affect your treatment and teaching of pupils.

The lesson referred to above indicates the importance of having a well-grounded pedagogy, and an informed understanding of how expectations impact on pupils' views of themselves and how, to a large extent, they dictate the level at which pupils perform. It is unfortunate that low expectations can lead teachers into working towards what they see as the lowest common denominator in their classes, though without some form of differentiated approach even this may not be achievable by some pupils. This can then become a vicious circle of low expectations producing low levels of attainment leading to even lower expectations on the part of both teachers and pupils. Where it is compounded by the ways in which pupils hear themselves talked about, both directly to their faces and between teachers, this is a deadly combination.

EFFECT OF EXPECTATIONS ON PUPILS' PERFORMANCE

A very simple way to show yourself the centrality of expectations in all classroom interactions, and of most pupil behaviour and performance, is to reconsider what you have probably already recognized during your time in schools: classes behave differently, and perform differently, according to the class teacher they are with. The question for you to consider is: how and why does this come about? To enable you to increase your understanding of how this happens, you might take the opportunity offered during your training to follow a class for a day, and to compare the ways in which the pupils performed in different lessons.

Other experiences will no doubt also offer you some useful ways of answering these questions. In addition, you might think about the following:

- How are pupils likely to feel about a lesson in which they know that they will never be challenged (even if they cannot articulate this response)?
- How are pupils likely to react in lessons which convey negative attitudes to them and their learning?
- How are pupils likely to react to a focus on their behaviour rather than on their learning?
- How do pupils respond to teachers who are clearly not interested?
- What approaches taken by teachers you have observed, or that you have used yourself, have engaged pupils' attention in a positive way?
- How was this achieved? What language and strategies were deployed by the teacher to keep pupil engagement high?
- How do pupils react when success in tests or examinations is used as a motivator?
- What kinds of classroom interactions appear to result in greater engagement by the pupils?
- What kinds of learning do these interactions make possible?

You are encouraged to draw working conclusions from these observations, which can be open to modification as you proceed. You should make detailed notes of all your answers and observations, in order to build up evidence for the good practice you have observed. Eventually, you should aim consciously to use these models in your teaching; they will obviously need to be an integral part of your lesson planning.

EXPECTATIONS OF SEN PUPILS

Teachers' expectations of pupils designated as having special educational needs (SEN) are automatically different from their expectations of other pupils. On the whole, expectations are lower and narrower, teaching is based on a reductive version of the curriculum and gives rise to class work which often does very little to stretch these pupils. There are several legitimate reasons for this, among them the lack of training for teaching SEN pupils, the lack of classroom support, the lack of suitable resources and funding and the perceived impossibility of coping with SEN pupils as well as the rest of a class.[1] On the other hand, this also demonstrates the effect on teacher expectations of the labels given to pupils, and teachers' reluctance and inability to ignore them, or at the very least question them and aim beyond them.

SEN pupils and their treatment in schools represent a potentially huge area for discussion, which not only encompasses considerations of what is meant by special educational needs, and of the whole edifice which has been constructed to cater for SEN pupils, but also involves consideration of the inclusion requirement of the National Curriculum and its implications. You are encouraged to address both these concepts (special educational needs and the pupils designated as having them, and inclusion) during the course of your career, and to work towards drawing your own conclusions about them on which to base your classroom and pedagogical practice. You are urged not to fall into the common position of undervaluing SEN pupils.[2]

During your training year you will undoubtedly encounter a range of approaches to the teaching of SEN pupils and will also learn about the Code of Practice governing the treatment and teaching of such pupils in mainstream schools. You are advised to take the opportunity of this year to establish an understanding of SEN pupils and their differing needs by close observation, and by talking to teachers, classroom assistants, SENCOs and the pupils themselves. It is also advised that you find out how your school caters for the range of needs, how support staff are deployed and how to develop your expertise in working with support staff during your teaching.

In terms of classroom evidence, you are encouraged to observe closely how one or two SEN pupils within a bigger class:

- respond to the work they are asked to do;
- work with the support they are given in the classroom;
- demonstrate that they have learned something;
- behave generally;

- volunteer to be involved in oral work of any kind;
- manage tasks involving reading and writing.

This exercise can also be carried out with a whole class in which all the pupils have SEN.

You are also encouraged to evaluate the expectations of SEN pupils demonstrated by teachers through noting:

- the way they speak about these pupils;
- the way they address these pupils;
- the matching, or otherwise, of lessons to pupils' needs;
- the way they interact with SEN pupils during the course of a lesson, in terms of encouragement, moving pupils on intellectually, developing skills;
- the preparation evident in the lesson, including pre-lesson planning with support staff.

It is also worth finding out the criteria by which the school has designated pupils as having special educational needs, especially if these pupils do not have a formal statement of educational need. Pupils falling into this category in any school are likely to meet a variety of teaching approaches and it is also the case that pupils put into SEN groups in one school might be grouped quite differently in other schools. Again, it is advisable to note down your findings, in order that you can consider their implications, and draw conclusions for your own practice from them.

EXPECTATIONS OF 'GIFTED AND TALENTED' PUPILS

The designation 'gifted and talented' came into use as a result of a recognition that many pupils were not stretched and challenged sufficiently to allow them to reach the higher levels of attainment of which they were deemed capable. The coinage is intended to cover the kinds of 'abilities' and potential demonstrated across a wide range of skills and achievement by the best pupils. The requirement laid on schools to address the 'different needs' of such pupils has reinforced the culture of individualization currently being fostered by central government and has laid even more responsibilities on teachers to be responsive to 'individual need' in their planning and teaching.

In contrast to the low level of expectation held of SEN pupils, it is frequently the case[3] that excessively high expectations are held of 'gifted and talented' pupils, but that this applies across a narrow range of achievement, such as literacy and numeracy. Expectations can be so high that teachers make inappropriate assumptions about what such pupils can already do and understand, and can leave them floundering because of inadequate support and explanation. This inconsistency in expectation between SEN pupils and 'gifted and talented' pupils illustrates the effect of labels: both their power to produce strong assumptions and expectations, and their power to limit fresh thinking. You are encouraged to apply the same investigative approaches to the treatment by your school of 'gifted and talented pupils' as of SEN pupils.

EFFECT OF EXPECTATIONS ON PUPILS' VIEWS OF THEMSELVES

Alongside teachers' expectations, pupils' expectations of themselves are of key importance to the success of classroom interactions.[4] High attaining pupils usually arrive in Year 7 full of enthusiasm and curiosity with a strong motivation and desire to learn. Their expectations, both of themselves and of what they will be asked to do, are high, and depending on a wide range of circumstance (including parental support and teacher attitudes) are likely to remain so. However, many lower attaining pupils arrive in Year 7 with very low expectations of themselves, often the result of the experiences they have had during their primary schooling. They are also likely to know their Key Stage 2 SATs results in English, mathematics and science, and these grades may have contributed to a low sense of self-worth. You are encouraged to try to see this from the pupils' viewpoint and to consider how they might feel as learners in school if most of the messages they have received about themselves so far have been negative. There is no doubt that pupils' expectations of themselves, just like adults', are central to everything which they do, attempt to do or refuse to do.

Less successful pupils' expectations of themselves are evident in more subtle ways than simply failing to 'do the work'. For example, they often demonstrate little or no concern that they may not have understood the content of the lesson, largely because they do not expect to, and often demonstrate very low expectations about the standard of their writing, both in terms of legibility and in terms of grammatical accuracy, and hand in work which falls far below the norm for their age. This sense of worthlessness and pointlessness can be compounded by a systematic lack of positive response by teachers to what pupils have produced (for example, negative marking or marking which has not been done), thus conveying lack of expectation in a particularly negative way, and it is therefore hardly surprising that some pupils take no pains with their work and display no understanding of why it matters.

The word 'work', which I have been using here, also highlights an area of real concern in the general attitudes to teaching in England, and this links in closely with a consideration of expectations. The connotations of the word 'work' – labour, toil, earning one's daily bread – may not be the most appropriate to be applied to what we are asking pupils to engage in at school. You are encouraged to think about shifting your mental vocabulary, with regard to what you want pupils to do, from 'work' to 'learning'. The word 'work' in lessons conjures up a typical lesson pattern, in which both teacher and pupils use 'work' to denote what pupils are 'doing', and from which any overt, discussed grasp of pupils' learning anything is conspicuously absent. This familiar pattern proceeds as follows:

- teacher introduces the lesson, explains the content, demonstrates or models, has some interchanges with pupils about it, possibly including questions;
- pupils settle down to the task and do their 'work';
- teacher takes in the books at the end of the lesson and marks the 'work';
- pupils may or may not receive back their 'work', possibly marked, at some future date when it may or may not have any remembered connection with new 'work'.

Repetitive lessons of this kind do little to disrupt pupils' expectations of themselves, and on the whole they merely confirm pupils' existing views. Where 'work' is never explicitly linked to learning, and therefore expectations are simply about completing tasks, pupils can be forgiven for having no real idea of where they are going in terms of any learning expected of them.

EFFECT OF IDEAS ABOUT ABILITY ON TEACHERS' EXPECTATIONS[5]

The idea of 'ability' has a long historical provenance, most notably its use as a term and concept of differentiation allowing the segregation of pupils into grammar, technical and secondary modern schools under the terms of the 1944 Education Act, on the basis of their performance in so-called 'intelligence tests' or more recently 'verbal reasoning tests'. While the intentions of the Act might have been conveyed as wholly benign (placing pupils in the type of school they were most fitted for according to their results in the 11+ examination), the subsequent effects were not so benign, and the negative sense of self-worth and loss of confidence brought about in many individuals by 'failing the 11+' lasted throughout their lives. You may know someone who experienced this; it would be worth your while to talk to them about their feelings, how they subsequently performed at the school to which they were sent, and whether ambitions they had as children were ever realized and whether their life chances were altered. This may help you see that the link between expectations, judgements about ability and sense of self-worth is very tight, and needs to be well understood by teachers.

Currently, the use of the term 'ability' remains largely unexamined in terms of what is meant by it. It is a common, if simplistic, way of categorizing pupils in order that they can be put into 'suitable sets'. Judgements are made about pupils' 'ability' according to a range of test results, including all the Key Stage SATs, reading tests administered at the start of Year 7, and sometimes also on the basis of teachers' assessments. Some subject teachers at secondary level are much more determined than others that they will not teach pupils other than in sets, and produce whole ranges of arguments about why this is the case.

This position, of course, tends to ignore the fact that sets are not themselves homogeneous in terms of what pupils in them are able to achieve, and so pupils have to be 'moved up' or 'moved down' when they perform above or below the norm expected for that set. It is worth considering your own position on this: do you subscribe to the idea of sets? in whose interests do you think they exist? why might many teachers favour the setting of pupils?

Other educational systems might regard the English concern with ability, and by extension with setting, to be antithetical to learning and education: a Soviet psychologist, writing after the death in 1934 of Lev Vygotsky,[6] wrote: 'Western researchers are constantly seeking to discover how the child came to be what he is. We in Russia are striving to discover not how the child came to be what he is, but how he can become what he is not yet.' You might like to consider the implications of this attitude in terms of what might be going on in classrooms. The antithesis suggested by this, between seeing the potential in each child on the one hand, and the innate 'inability' of children to move much beyond the point at which they have already arrived on the other, is worth thinking about. In this connection it is also useful to consider what you know from experience about the capacity of children to learn, even if you have not yet given this a great deal of thought. At a very simple level, think about what most children have achieved by the age of five[7]:

- speech, including the ability to use past, present and future tenses, to be generally accurate with verb agreements and prepositions, to know and use at least 4,000 words, to read and write at a basic level;
- ability to listen and converse;
- ability to listen to stories, poems and music, and show preferences;
- development of imagination;
- development of emotional responses, including the ability to empathize;
- ability to guess, predict, consider the past, remember, speculate, estimate;
- ability to reason, evaluate, consider, compare, prefer, desire;
- understanding rules, conditions, rewards, punishments;

- a very wide range of motor skills, including all the operations involved in playing, constructing, drawing, painting, running, jumping, swimming, walking, knowing left from right, singing, dancing.

This extraordinary rate of learning, which is usually achieved as a matter of course, suggests that in optimum circumstances the human brain is capable of learning without limits. Unfortunately, optimum circumstances rarely exist. Nevertheless, even within the constraints operating on children both within and outside school, children's learning is capable of being developed far beyond what is routinely expected of them. The notion of 'ability' becomes increasingly questionable when placed in this kind of context. Consider a system of teaching which:

> . . . is intended to outpace the child's development, and is supposed to be pitched at such a level that it will bring the child on from the position s/he has reached to that s/he can potentially reach, given the help of the teacher. It is the task of the teacher to fill this zone and that of the methodologist to help the teacher find the right method in order to fill it. Thus the weak child has greater, not less 'potential' than the bright one, because the zone of next development is larger.[8]

You are invited to give this proposition some thought, and to compare it with the following simplified account of what the application of judgements and measurements of 'ability' usually results in in schools in England. As a general rule, beliefs about 'ability' have produced a common terminology and set of understandings subscribed to by most teachers and schools:

- high ability = top set
- average ability = middle set
- low ability = bottom set

The notion of top, middle and bottom sets triggers an automatic, unexamined response in many teachers, which centres on levels of expectation. No matter what the nature of a school's overall intake, for most teachers the promise of working with a 'top set' means that they can 'really' get going in 'teaching' their subject, and they are likely to have very high, often misplaced, expectations of these pupils. It is not uncommon to hear such teachers express incomprehension about a so-called 'top set' in a middle ranking school being unable to do something which they assumed they would be able to do.

'Ability' means different things in different schools, depending on their intake. A so-called 'high ability' pupil in one school might be only of 'average ability' in another, or even labelled 'low ability' in another. The term is, in other words, highly slippery and can clearly never be *absolutely* defined. This might help you to begin unpicking this term for yourself and, as a start, consider which of the following meanings is generally ascribed to the term in the English education system:

- a finite quantity of 'ability' with which each pupil is endowed?

or

- a stage of development, from which pupils can and will move on?

Something like the first definition is used by most schools as the basis of their judgements; that is, on the whole, pupils have been endowed with 'ability' to a greater or lesser degree, and it is the school's job to provide some kind of an education which will suit that level of 'ability'. This belief system does not preclude developing pupils' skills, understanding and knowledge, but it does imply that there are firm limits to what individuals will be able to achieve.

The second definition implies a rather different way of looking at pupils, learning and development, more in line with the Russian approach outlined in the quotation above. It is based on an understanding that ability is not a finite quantity, that pupils develop at different rates and that pupils' inability to do something at one stage of their lives does not mean that they will never be able to do it. Such an understanding indicates a rather different attitude to children in general, and is clearly concerned with moving children on without limit rather than consigning them to a reductive curriculum which is deemed to cater for their 'ability'.

You may already have been thinking about this, and it is important that you should continue to do so: *ability*, and teachers' understanding of what it means, is the basis of most school organization. It determines sets and set sizes, teacher allocation to classes, the use of classroom and other assistants, the focus on test and examination results, and the level of GCSE examination for which pupils will be entered, and therefore taught. As a marker of expectations about pupils, the label *ability* focuses on what they can already do rather than on where they might be led to in the future. It would be useful to you to find out which secondary subjects in your practice school routinely use setting as a means of organizing pupils for teaching purposes, and which do not, and if possible talk to some of the teachers involved about their views of setting.

In this regard, it is also sensible to keep in mind the notion of the self-fulfilling prophecy, and to remember that pupils are well aware of where they have been placed in setting systems, of how they are regarded, and of the levels of expectation held about them, and perform accordingly.

EFFECT ON TEACHING OF DIFFERENT LEVELS OF EXPECTATION

Within the current system, in which the currency of 'ability' dominates thinking about pupils' learning and achievement, it is hardly surprising that many teachers have a strong professional investment in being given 'top' sets to teach. This validates their idea of themselves as 'teachers', accords status within departments and the school as a whole, and if their pupils are consistently successful in reaching the desired levels at GCSE, can determine career and salary prospects. Being given 'bottom sets' (often labelled 'low ability' sets) is generally not popular, and is often a kind of punishment meted out to teachers regarded as not pulling their weight. The needs of pupils in these sets are not seen as a priority. The pressure on schools to produce the maximum percentages of A–C passes at GCSE has a commensurately negative effect on the opportunities offered to such pupils, and serves to confirm an already existing bias against them.

If you have the opportunity during your training, observe the ways in which teachers prepare for and approach the teaching of different sets, and if possible talk to them about their views of their pupils. Try to draw conclusions from this, particularly about your own attitudes and future approaches. It is important that you think through your position with regard to the above, particularly as you are aiming to be a successful secondary teacher. Now is the time to recognize and accept that your responsibility as a teacher is to *all* the pupils you are asked to teach, and that all of them need the benefit of the expertise that you will be able to deploy. Your acquisition of the skills and pedagogical and methodological understanding necessary for supporting the development of all pupils will be helped by later chapters.

SUMMARY

In addition to the thinking you have been invited to do as a result of reading this chapter, it is also suggested that you:

- observe one or two SEN pupils for a lesson, using the guidelines given;
- find out the criteria used by the school in designating non-statemented pupils as SEN;
- talk to someone you know who failed the 11+ about their feelings;
- talk to teachers about their views of setting;
- talk to teachers about their views of the pupils in different levels of set.

STANDARDS

This chapter will support and develop your thinking about issues implicit in the following standards. Trainees:

1.1;   have high expectations of all pupils; respect their social, cultural, linguistic, religious and ethnic backgrounds; and are committed to raising their educational achievement;

1.2;   treat pupils consistently, with respect and consideration, and are concerned for their development as learners;

1.6;   understand the contribution that support staff and other professionals make to teaching and learning;

2.6;   understand their responsibilities under the *SEN Code of Practice* and know how to seek advice from specialists on less common types of special educational need;

3.1.1; set challenging teaching and learning objectives which are relevant to all pupils in their classes. They base these on their knowledge of: the pupils' evidence of their past and current achievement; the expected standards for pupils of the relevant age range; the range and content of work relevant to pupils in that age range;

3.3.1; have high expectations of pupils and build successful relationships, centred on teaching and learning. They establish a purposeful learning environment where diversity is valued and where pupils feel secure and confident.

NOTES

1 Lawson, H. (2005),'Understandings of inclusion: the perceptions of teachers and teaching assistants'. *The Times Educational Supplement*. Obtainable from: h.lawson@plymouth.ac.uk.

2 A recent article in *The Times Educational Supplement* (12 August 2005), reporting on an address to a conference of special needs experts, quotes the speaker (Elias Avramidis of York University) as saying that when talking in public about special needs pupils, teachers used appropriate terms, but in the staffroom such children are often referred to as 'nutters' or 'hooligans'. 'Promoting inclusive education from expertism to sustainable inclusive practices' is obtainable from: ea13@york.ac.uk.

3 Smith, C. (2005) 'Paradigm shifts in inclusive and gifted education'. *The Times Educational Supplement*. Obtainable from: C.Smith@educ.gla.ac.uk.

4 London Institute of Education (2005), 'A systematic review of what pupils, aged 11–16, believe impacts on their motivation to learn in the classroom'. Obtainable from http://eppi.ioe.ac.uk.

5 A good resource for this topic is Hart, S. *et al.* (2004), *Learning Without Limits*. Maidenhead: Open University Press.

6 The author of the seminal work *Thought and Language*, first written in the 1930s, which emphasized the strong connection between children's language and the development of their thinking.

7 Donaldson, M. (1992), *Human Minds: An exploration*. London: Allen Lane.

8 Muckle, J. (1998), *A Guide to the Soviet Curriculum: What the Russian child is taught in school*. London: Croom Helm.

Chapter 3

Pupils' needs

In this chapter, various needs exhibited by pupils are discussed in a general way, in order to bring them to your attention. The needs discussed here do not take account of the specific needs of pupils with SEN, or of pupils with disabilities, though some of their needs inevitably fall within those identified here.

Attempting to realize the concept of 'individual needs' with regard to teaching pupils within an education system could be regarded as impossibly idealistic, and susceptible to innumerable difficulties. As a concept it is somewhat elastic in terms of what it actually means. It raises questions about levels and systems of diagnosis, the necessary levels of expertise to address diagnosed needs, and the ability of any school to operate with the degree of flexibility implied.

Nevertheless, it is necessary to consider the likely range of needs represented in any class of pupils. Very often these will not be particular to only one or two individuals, in which case it is much easier to build in ways of addressing these needs in your planning. Where needs are quite obviously demonstrated by individuals only, you may find that you can plan to meet them by working collaboratively with a teaching assistant, or other member of staff who can support the individuals on a one-to-one basis. If a pupil has really intrusive individual needs, over and above any demonstrated by other members of the class, you are likely to require different strategies, starting with consultation with colleagues, the head of department and head of year. As with everything else you do in school, you do need to know what the school's policies are in relation to this area.

The rest of this chapter discusses the following needs likely to be demonstrated by some of the pupils you teach:

- language needs;
- skills needs;
- behaviour modification needs.

LANGUAGE NEEDS

You can usefully also consider language needs in relation to the section on Literacy across the Curriculum which is discussed in Chapter 5. As a simplification, it is possible to broadly categorize pupils' language needs as follows:

- Lack of familiarity with the language conventions commonly deployed in schools, both at institutional and at classroom level – these can include instructions, commands, the language of discipline, public language such as that used in assemblies, letters to parents and teachers' classroom language.
- As yet unable to read with understanding the texts used in lessons.
- As yet lacking the expected range of writing skills.
- Lacking confidence and fluency in speaking.
- Still acquiring English, as an additional language, and therefore attempting to operate in an alien context.
- Fluent in English, but mainly speaking another language at home.
- Bringing different cultural and language experiences into school.
- Having language needs linked to specific disabilities, such as hearing impairment.

Some suggestions are now given to help you cope with the implicit challenges inherent in these needs, and to encourage you to accept that addressing these needs is the responsibility of every teacher.

Lack of familiarity with language conventions deployed in schools as a whole

This is far more common than is often recognized, and is probably best dealt with during form time. Attention is rarely given on a whole-school basis to the problems caused by this lack of understanding, which can be very common in schools with large minority ethnic intakes, including the children of asylum seekers. Words, phrases and references which teachers take for granted can be completely baffling to pupils, especially those new to the school. The nomenclature used at secondary level, which pupils will not have met in their primary schools, includes: *forms, sets, form time, break, lessons, timetables, the different rooms in the school, the ever-increasing number of acronyms used in education (PSHE, GCSE, GNVQ, A level, G and T, SEN are some examples), examinations, the specialized vocabulary of each subject area* and so on. In the case of newly arrived pupils, it is important that you recognize in your preparation and teaching that they will need focused help. Obviously, pupils learn these things as they go along, but it is the mark of a good teacher that s/he ensures that pupils are not left floundering.

Unable to read with understanding

This is far more common than is often realized. Pupils are expected to be able to negotiate the meanings of subject-based texts, and then derive understanding and factual knowledge from them without necessarily having the range of reading skills which will allow them to do this success-fully. You are encouraged to recognize that this is likely to be the case with some of the pupils in each of your classes, and to consider how you will help them. The first point to consider is whether the text you are using could be dispensed with altogether, and whether you could not convey the same content in a much more understandable way yourself. It is also sensible to consider the kind of learning interaction you are expecting the text to bring about. The reading challenges posed by texts for many pupils do need serious consideration on your part; one productive and positive way of doing this is to devote some time at the start of a lesson to getting pupils to become the analysts of the text you are proposing to use.

Essentially, you need to consider the advantages and disadvantages of using texts in relation to the time you have available, the learning outcomes you are aiming for and the reading skills levels of your pupils. The more detailed advice given in Chapter 5 about Literacy across the Curriculum should also be consulted here.

Lacking writing skills

It is advisable not to assume that pupils can write at the level you are planning for before you have actually found out. It is also advisable that you learn how to teach the specific writing skills needed in your subject area, which will include spelling, sentencing, paragraphing, other ways of dividing up text, writing in different styles and for different purposes, the stylistic conventions of different genre types, for example *narrative, recording, recounting, describing, reporting.* With pupils whose writing is still undeveloped, you will need to give them opportunities to record their thoughts in other ways, possibly through a peer writing for them, or by giving them simplified templates. You do have a responsibility to develop your pupils' literacy skills, whatever your subject area.

Lacking confidence and fluency in speaking

The best thing you can do for such pupils is to devise teaching approaches which place a great deal of emphasis on speaking and listening, and thereby encourage such pupils to participate in lessons with greater confidence. All pupils need opportunities to speak, discuss, share and explore through speaking and listening, and the more you can build this into your lesson planning the better. The connection between spoken confidence and speaking opportunities and the development of pupils' higher order thinking skills has been shown in some important research studies[1] and it is important to bear this in mind as you plan for teaching your classes. For pupils lacking confidence, you should use methods which do not show them up, but which nevertheless give them the support to speak out with confidence. It is noticeable that many pupils have poor levels of spoken articulacy, and consequently low levels of confidence when they are expected to speak in front of the class, or in any other more public forum.

Still acquiring English

Pupils still acquiring English tend to fall into one of two categories: newly arrived children, who are often asylum seekers; and those who were born here but have not spoken English until they started schooling. Pupils who are still acquiring English should ideally be taught separately to begin with, to give them better opportunities when they do join mainstream classes. However, it can be the case that you will find such pupils in one or more of your classes, and you will need to have some strategies for helping them. You may not always have a learning assistant. The school SENCO may have some suggestions but not necessarily, as working with pupils whose only educational need is to acquire English is not always part of mainstream thinking about SEN. Given the lack of specialized provision for such pupils in many schools, you may find yourself getting by as well as you can; the important thing is that you do something, and do not leave such pupils to struggle along as best they may. One observed feature of many such pupils is their very high level of commitment, and desire to learn.

Fluent in English, but speaking another language at home / bringing different cultural and language experiences into school

Pupils in this position in English schools, many of whom are speakers of Asian languages such as Punjabi, Urdu, Mirpuri and Sylheti, and increasingly of Eastern European and African languages, often unwittingly mislead teachers into thinking that they have understood more than they actually have, largely because their spoken English is fluent. As with all pupils, levels of understanding should not be taken for granted. With the pupils identified here, it is worth discussing the situation with them in a genuine spirit of enquiry, in order to find out whether they can point out those aspects of language used in your subject they have problems with. This is a far more productive approach, and far more likely to engage your pupils in your subject, than if you simply ignore this factor in your rush to get through the curriculum. Another area for simple research by your pupils is to get them to help you identify likely misunderstandings because of different cultural and religious assumptions.

It is also worth spending part of a lesson at the start of your time with a class in a simple language survey, so that all class members can recognize the range of language skills within the class as a whole. The survey might include all pupils noting:

- the language they speak at home;
- when they first started speaking English;
- the other languages they speak and when they use them;
- which languages they can read;
- which languages they can write;
- when they first learned to read, in any language;
- when they started to learn to write, in any language;
- the language/s they use with friends;
- the language/s they use with parents or other adults.

The survey can then branch out into drawing up a language help plan, so that pupils are paired with others who will help them with specific problems. You may think all this is the job of the English department, but a little thought will suggest that this is not so. In order for pupils to succeed in your subject area, you need to be the one who knows about their language strengths and needs.

Language needs associated with disabilities

Pupils with disabilities often have the support of a learning assistant, with whom you should expect to work closely as a matter of course. As the class teacher you should be aware of the needs of these pupils, and should ensure that your planning and preparation takes account of them. A simple example is the enlarging of printed or other text for pupils with visual impairment; another example is for you to use the special amplification system (a small radio microphone linked to a hearing aid) for pupils with hearing impairment. In all cases, you should consult the teachers with designated responsibility for these pupils, to ensure that you are doing everything necessary to develop their learning. It is important that you review and evaluate your teaching and your pupils' progress on a regular basis to ensure that you are not making assumptions about your pupils' levels of understanding.

SKILLS NEEDS

You will inevitably be involved in developing pupils' skills in relation to the subject you are teaching. It might be helpful to divide skills into two broad categories: *cognitive skills* and *motor skills.*

In considering *cognitive skills,* it is important to recognize the integral link between language, cognition and conceptualization. Pupils' grasp of the conceptual content of what they are engaged in learning is tightly connected to the language level at which they are operating. In some respects, therefore, it is not possible to separate cognitive skills from language skills; in order to understand and then be able to work with a concept, pupils need to be able to deploy the language through which the concept is expressed. From your point of view, you need to consider how well your planning for teaching is taking account of pupils' ability to engage with the cognitive and conceptual content of your lesson. Examples of pupils having problems in grasping the cognitive content of lessons exist in most subject areas. It is therefore important that you recognize the conceptual content of your lessons, and that you take steps to help pupils grasp it.

It is as important to recognize pupils' problems with *motor skills* as with language and cognitive skills. In subject areas where motor skills are most likely to be very visible, such as PE, it becomes very clear to teachers what pupils still have to learn. In other subject areas, lack of some motor skills may only show up in quite subtle ways. Pupils' ability to manipulate the physical tools used in different subject areas, such as those used in art, design and technology, music and the sciences, cannot be taken for granted by teachers, and obviously pupils in these areas are explicitly taught how to manage these tools. In subjects such as English, history and geography, where writing implements are the most common tool, pupils' difficulties in producing legible handwriting are often all too apparent. Insofar as writing by hand still remains the dominant method by which pupils communicate in writing, it is important that secondary teachers take some notice of the ways in which pupils write, and take steps to help them improve where needed. Appendix 3 offers more detailed advice on handwriting.

Finally, it is useful to remember that pupils' cognitive and intellectual development is highly dependent on the development of their motor skills, and that the artificial division between the mind and the body which has been a fundamental feature of Western thought and philosophy is not necessarily very helpful when it comes to educating children. The increasing attention being paid to the way in which the human brain works, and also to the ways in which the brain develops from birth, has resulted in research findings that are contributing in a fundamental way to current thinking about learning. Pioneering teachers working with disabled children have discovered, for example, that a focus on the development of motor skills (including movement, dance, playing musical instruments) produces a noticeable improvement in children's use of language and cognitive development. In another area, teachers working with mainstream pupils in many subject areas use drama and other physically active methods as a way of developing pupils' thinking, understanding and language skills. In some primary schools, teachers now routinely use short breaks in lessons for pupils to carry out some form of vigorous physical activity, in a controlled way, to stimulate their brains.

BEHAVIOURAL NEEDS

This section is entitled 'behavioural needs' because of the noticeable increase in the number of pupils who appear not to know how to comply with accepted norms of behaviour in schools and classrooms. Such pupils clearly have needs; they actually need to be taught how to behave appropriately. Many of their problems stem from their not having had clear, consistent boundaries for behaviour during their young lives so far. This does not mean that they have to be cowed into submission, but that they are helped to learn how to control their behaviour, and how to take responsibility within the boundaries set up and maintained by you, and within school as a whole. Working with such pupils requires you to set up and maintain clear boundaries.

Pupils generally exhibit many different behaviours in classrooms, some of which are contingent on the behaviour and expectations of the class teacher. Others, equally importantly, are generated by circumstances beyond the teacher's control, but are imported into the classroom for the teacher to deal with. It is important for you to have some basic understanding of what can produce inappropriate behaviours, and that you acquire some strategies for helping pupils overcome these barriers to their own learning.

Behaviours in response to teachers

As a generalization, it can be said that teachers who are seen by pupils to be:

- organized;
- purposeful;
- authoritative (*not* authoritarian);
- fair, considerate and consistent;
- supportive;

will tend to gain the trust and cooperation of their pupils. When pupils can see that the lesson has a clearly defined purpose, and can see its benefit for themselves, they are more likely to work with the teacher, and each other. When pupils cannot see what the lesson is for or about, or when the teacher is obviously uncertain, then pupils are more likely to go off task, and possibly misbehave. Once pupils sense hesitation on the part of the teacher, they are quite likely to make the lesson very difficult. Pupils also often misbehave when they are bored; it is therefore important that you ensure that the conceptual/thinking content of your lessons is high, and that you avoid imposing on your pupils repetitive tasks leading to little or no learning.

Pupils may also bring into your classroom the overspill from a previous lesson, or an incident with another teacher or pupil in the corridor or at break or lunch time and may not be able to control their behaviour for emotional reasons. Your informed understanding and knowledge of how to treat these incidents calmly and with dignity is important here.

Behaviours caused by external circumstances

Pupils, like the rest of us, are affected emotionally by everything that happens to them. Given the inexperience and lack of emotional maturity of many adolescents, it is hardly surprising that their failure to deal with emotional problems arising from events outside the classroom will affect their behaviour in lessons. This can be a difficult area for teachers to cope with, and can often lead to unnecessary confrontations between teachers and pupils. Secondary pupils often entirely lack the command of appropriate spoken language with which to respond to what teachers say, and are just as likely to resort to defensive aggression as to feel confident that teachers will handle their situation with sensitivity. What may sound like defiance, 'cheek' or rudeness is often the immature and clumsy expression of hurt feelings, frustration, lack of confidence and anger. You should be ready to accept your responsibility as an *adult* in working with pupils, and ensure that as their teacher, and as a professional, your role is to demonstrate to pupils behaviours other than those which have brought about confrontations in the first place.

It can be helpful to think through your attitudes to and expectations of pupils' behaviour in your lessons, and to be prepared to be flexible as well as consistent. To this end, it is a good idea to have a range of strategies to use when you are faced with unpredicted behaviour from your pupils. For example, when pupils come into your classroom after a wet and windy break time, they are highly likely to be unusually loud, noisy and possibly confrontational. A well-applied method for calming them all down, with understanding, will be far more effective than a dictatorial approach which shows no understanding of their mood. Behaviour and behaviour management are treated further in later chapters.

SUMMARY

It is suggested that in thinking about and analysing pupils' needs, you use the list below:

- work with learning assistants to plan for the needs of individual pupils;
- know school policies about the treatment of disruptive pupils.
- Build into your planning opportunities to help pupils with unfamiliar language;
- give careful consideration to the reading challenges posed by texts you aim to use: are they really necessary?
- do not make assumptions about the writing skills levels of pupils; teach them what they need to know for your subject, and pay attention to handwriting;
- plan into your lessons as many opportunities as possible for speaking and listening to develop pupils' confidence;
- discuss language and understanding with pupils, help them analyse their difficulties in grasping concepts;
- deal with behavioural incidents calmly and with dignity; model desired, adult behaviour.

STANDARDS

This chapter will help you think about and address issues implicit in the following standards. Trainees:

1.1; have high expectations of all pupils; respect their social, cultural, linguistic, religious and ethnic backgrounds; and are committed to raising their educational achievement;

1.2; treat pupils consistently, with respect and consideration, and are concerned for their development as learners;

1.3; demonstrate and promote the positive values, attitudes and behaviour that they expect from their pupils;

1.6; understand the contribution that support staff and other professionals make to teaching and learning;

1.7;   are able to improve their own teaching, by evaluating it and learning from the effective practice of others and from evidence;

2.4;   understand how pupils' learning can be affected by their physical, intellectual, linguistic, social, cultural and emotional development;

2.6;   understand their responsibilities under the *SEN Code of Practice* and know how to seek advice from specialists on less common types of special educational need;

2.7;   know a range of strategies to promote good behaviour and establish a purposeful learning environment;

3.3.2; can teach the required or expected knowledge, understanding and skills relevant to the curriculum for pupils in the age range for which they are trained;

3.3.4; differentiate their teaching to meet the needs of pupils, including the more able and those with special educational needs;

3.3.5; are able to support those who are learning English as an additional language (EAL);

3.3.13; work collaboratively with specialist teachers and other colleagues and, with the help of an experienced teacher as appropriate, manage the work of teaching assistants or other adults to enhance pupils' learning.

NOTE

1 For example Barnes, D., Britton, J. and Rosen, H. (1969), *Language, the Learner and the School*. Harmondsworth: Penguin Books; Barnes, D. and Todd, F. (1995), *Communication and Learning Revisited: Making meaning through talk*. London: Heinemann; Edwards, A. D. and Westgate, D. P. G. (1994), *Investigating Classroom Talk* (2nd edn). London: Falmer Press; and Corden, R. (2000), *Literacy and Learning through Talk*. Buckingham: Open University Press.

Chapter 4

The National Curriculum and subject knowledge

The National Curriculum did not suddenly introduce the idea of curricular demands into secondary subject teaching; teaching at this level had already been constrained by the demands of 16+ and A level examination syllabuses, and most schools worked with internally set syllabuses of one kind or another, even if these were somewhat generalized. However, the pre-National Curriculum era did undoubtedly give teachers rather more freedom for teaching decisions than they currently enjoy. This chapter is intended to provide you with a critical viewpoint from which to consider the National Curriculum, and to make general links with your subject knowledge.

THE ARTIFICIALITY OF THE SECONDARY APPROACH TO LEARNING AND 'SUBJECTS'

The existing curriculum as taught in secondary schools in England is mostly a derivative of nineteenth-century thinking about education. Put simply, this is based on the categorization approach to knowledge and understanding, and also on ideas of learning as a linear activity, as well as on ideas of what children of different social classes needed to know and be able to do. For us in the twenty-first century, it is becoming clear that the increasingly sophisticated use of Information and Communications Technology (ICT) by pupils and teachers both at home and in school, as well as fundamental changes in employment opportunities and work patterns, is throwing into question these earlier, subject-based models of what a curriculum should look like. However, you are likely to continue to be expected to teach your 'subject', and you will also have trained to teach your 'subject', so this short section is inviting you to consider the implications of this in terms of pupils' grasp of the world around them. A critique of current practice might include the following:

- pupils are taught, overtly or otherwise, that their learning approach is going to be expected to be different according to which subject they are being taught; this means that they are not automatically helped to develop as autonomous, conscious learners, but are subjected to the different expectations of different teachers;
- pupils are not encouraged to see connections between subjects, which they regard as inhabiting separate boxes (and classrooms) and indeed can be quite shocked when a teacher displays knowledge of another subject area;
- pupils are unlikely to gain an overview of the interrelatedness of knowledge and experiences;
- Teachers tend to see themselves as teachers of subjects rather than as teachers of pupils;
- the subject-based curriculum carries strong status connotations, with academic subjects still accorded much higher status than practical subjects;
- the subject-based curriculum encourages, even expects, pupils to be 'better' at some subjects than others, and uses this to push them in certain post-16 and post-18 directions; this ensures that pupils also see themselves in this way;
- the subject-based curriculum does little to help pupils overcome their beliefs that ability in subjects is genetically determined, as in 'I can't spell, but that's because my mum can't either';
- the subject-based curriculum, and its accompanying testing and examinations regime, tends to narrow the focus in subject areas and to place arbitrary limits on pupils' learning;

- the subject-based curriculum tends to encourage teachers to lower their expectations of what pupils can achieve.

The fragmentary effect of curriculum organization and approaches based on 'subjects' is exacerbated by the so-called modular approach, exemplified in much of the syllabus for GNVQs, so that the increasingly observable outcome is pupils' inability and unwillingness to make links and to be prepared to think 'outside the box'.

THE NATIONAL CURRICULUM

You will probably have been introduced to the National Curriculum very early on in your training course; it is, naturally, the dominant piece of documentation underpinning your training, and it will be familiar to you as an organizational, curricular tool, and as a set of requirements to which you know you must adhere. It is likely that you will rarely, if ever, have serious opportunities to critique the National Curriculum during your career, though you will probably have some opportunities to do so during your training year.

The imposition of the National Curriculum on the state education system (independent schools are exempt from its requirements, though many choose to follow them) in the late 1980s needs to be understood from several perspectives:

- the ostensible purposes for its introduction;
- the centralized control over education implicit in a National Curriculum;
- the methods used to ensure that it is implemented in schools;
- its implied pedagogy;
- its effect on teachers.

The ostensible purpose for the introduction of a National Curriculum was to ensure that no matter where pupils were being educated within the state system, and no matter how many times they might move schools for whatever reason, they would by and large receive the same curriculum. There was much emphasis at the time on pupils' 'entitlements', and much of the pressure on teachers and schools in the years following its introduction was to ensure that pupils received their 'entitlement'.

It was recognized at the time, however, and has become increasingly clear over the years, that the National Curriculum is in fact a method of controlling not only what teachers teach, but to a large extent how they teach it. The actual National Curriculum specifications for each subject area throughout the Key Stages were arrived at as a result of the deliberations of subject working parties; the composition of these varied, but teachers were poorly represented on many of them, and therefore in many ways teachers as a body were excluded from the radical decision-making inherent in framing such a curriculum. Subsequently, the National Curriculum has been supported in its implementation and pedagogy by a plethora of government strategies, initiatives, the National Strategy and further demands placed on schools, such as the teaching of citizenship.

To ensure that schools and teachers were complying with the demands of the National Curriculum and with the demands of a vigorously advocated notion of 'parental choice', a range of measures was imposed, including the publication of league tables in the local and national press to show how schools were performing in 16+ examinations, the reshaping of Her Majesty's Inspectorate for Schools (HMI) into the Office for Standards in Education (Ofsted), and the clear duty laid on local authorities to train their teachers in compliance with curriculum requirements. The publication of league tables, accompanied by changes in the ways schools' intakes are managed, on the basis of parental choice rather than local catchment areas, has ensured that what schools do is constantly in the public eye, and constantly available for a high level of public scrutiny, often of an entirely uninformed kind.

The implied pedagogy underpinning the teaching of the National Curriculum is vague; 'pupils should be taught' is the directive for all subject areas, followed by a list of desired content and skills. Supporting materials have offered suggestions about how some of this teaching could be carried out, but more support has been offered at the planning and organizational level than at the pedagogical level. For example, much of the framing of the National Curriculum was connected to ideas of what pupils 'ought to be able to do', but little if any of it was concerned to unpick its pedagogical implications. The organizational suggestions were often about schemes of work through which the prescriptive programmes of study could be realized, to the extent that in most subject departments in most schools, schemes of work have been devised which offer teachers a framework (or often a support) for their teaching. Planning schemes of work can require a lot of time and effort; it is not surprising that once they have been completed teachers are reluctant to have to do them all over again.

The effect on teachers of this weight of obligation and expectation has by and large been to close down exploratory discussion of what each subject is or should be about, in favour of discussion about how to implement the requirements of the National Curriculum, the National Strategy and examination specifications. In addition, teachers are constantly aware of having to work to a centralized agenda, making continuously new demands on them, and often in situations where their best intentions for their pupils are thwarted by externally imposed requirements.

The opportunities for serious debate about what our education system is for, which could have been taken up as part of the framing of the National Curriculum, were eschewed in favour of a narrowly conceived, instrumental curriculum, devised to cater for the opinions and expectations of employers, opinionated journalists, uninformed and biased politicians and ambitious parents. It is, for example, noteworthy that the curriculum for history should be decided by a Secretary of State for Education for political rather than educational reasons.

Common requirements of the National Curriculum

The National Curriculum for all subjects is divided into the same two broad categories: *Knowledge, skills and understanding*; and *Breadth of study*. To encourage you to be informed about the likely content and range of study that your pupils will be following in their other subject lessons, a brief digest of the curriculum for most subjects is given in Appendix 2.

The range of skills which you could expect your pupils to have developed during their Key Stage 3 years, before they make choices for GCSE courses, are listed below. There is a significant commonality across most subject areas prescribed for by the National Curriculum in requiring pupils to be able to:

- select and apply;
- evaluate;
- investigate;
- consider evidence;
- interpret;
- enquire;
- communicate;
- discuss.

It would be sensible to inform yourself of how colleagues in both your own and other subject areas help their pupils acquire the prescribed range of skills. You might be tempted to regard these skills as being *in addition* to what you have to teach by way of cognitive subject content, but these are clearly all *embedded skills*: without the ability to deploy them, pupils will not be able to engage fully in the demands of the curriculum as a whole. It could be argued, therefore, that your subject knowledge is not just about what you know in relation to your chosen subject, but that it also includes knowledge about how to enable your pupils to deploy the skills through which their learning of subject knowledge will be demonstrated.

Planning for teaching the National Curriculum is a real challenge with regard to ensuring that pupils are being given their entitlement. The sheer scope and detail of requirements in most subject areas are quite impossible for many pupils to take in, and quite impossible for teachers to teach so that all pupils in all classes learn what is laid down. This rather overloaded system means that very often teachers 'cover' the requirements, and have little time to actually ensure that pupils are learning anything. It is worth considering the following:

- Is it better to 'get through' the syllabus, according to a pre-planned programme, irrespective of pupils' ability to learn anything from it?
or:

- Is it better to ensure that all pupils learn and understand, even if this means going more slowly, and not covering the whole syllabus?

You are encouraged to give careful thought to these two alternatives, and to consider whether you have already observed either of them in practice in your school.

SUBJECT KNOWLEDGE AND THE NATIONAL CURRICULUM

The National Curriculum subject working parties were faced with the question: what do teachers in each subject area need to know in order to teach their subject? The question applied as much at primary as at secondary level, with the tacit understanding that each individual primary teacher would need to acquire, or have, all the subject knowledge required across the whole curriculum for the primary phase, whereas secondary teachers would need only to have the knowledge specified for their subject at secondary level.

The National Curriculum in some respects solved the problem by specifying what should be taught in each subject area (in the process generating fierce debate about the ways in which these specifications had been arrived at) and thereby also specified by implication what teachers of each subject needed to know. A later incarnation of these requirements (since abandoned), designed for teacher trainers and trainees, sought to make as clear as possible what each trainee needed to know about their subject in order to be awarded Qualified Teacher Status (QTS).

SUBJECT KNOWLEDGE: YOUR STARTING POINT

In many ways your subject knowledge will be individual to you; your understanding of the subject which you wish to teach is only likely to be shared by others in a fairly broad way. Your uniqueness, while in itself much to be welcomed and applauded, does make for difficulties when you start to look at the National Curriculum for Key Stages 3, 4 and 5, and realize that you may have to learn a great deal more than you already know in order to feel confident about teaching your subject. During your training year, therefore, you will need to be prepared to learn aspects of your subject which you do not already know, while at the same time learning how to transform that knowledge into lesson content which your pupils can engage in.

You might begin by considering the following questions:

- What is a 'subject'?
- What constitutes 'knowledge' of a subject?
- Is the notion of subject knowledge, and the requirement that trainee teachers, and indeed teachers, show that they have it, likely to lead to particular kinds of classroom interactions?
- Could the requirement laid on trainees to acquire the specified subject knowledge result in a narrowing of focus and interest, and a subsequent loss of wider views and experiences being brought to bear in teaching?
- What is your opinion of what the National Curriculum specifies for your subject?

One of the fundamental challenges you will face as you learn to become a teacher is the transformation of your existing knowledge, including the new knowledge and understanding you acquire during your training, into something that you can teach. In very simple terms, you will have to learn how to change knowledge you acquired as a *learner* into knowledge which you can use as a *teacher*. This process involves a radical change in the direction of your thinking, and in your understanding of this knowledge. It also requires a change of focus from yourself to the pupils you will be teaching. This sounds self-evident, but trainees at the start of their training year are often very unsure about this process of reformulation and refocusing, and take time to learn how to successfully use their own subject knowledge for the benefit of their pupils.

Developing your subject knowledge will involve you in:

- extending what you already know;
- transforming what you already know into content which you can teach.

EXTENDING WHAT YOU ALREADY KNOW

It is unlikely that you are familiar with everything in the curriculum for your subject area, and you will therefore need to devise ways which suit you to acquire the knowledge you do not have. Your ITT course and the experiences you have in school will contribute to this further acquisition of subject knowledge. In addition you should be prepared to undertake a lot of reading and subject-based research in order that you can teach your subject up to A level. Very skilled and experienced teachers do sometimes take a different approach: instead of arming themselves with as much knowledge as possible, they openly discuss with their pupils the knowledge that is required and devise ways in which teacher and pupils can learn together. This can lead to extremely fruitful learning experiences, in which pupils are given much greater responsibility for their learning than if the teacher already 'knows' it all.

KNOWING HOW TO TURN YOUR TEACHER KNOWLEDGE INTO LEARNER KNOWLEDGE

This is a very challenging aspect of your training, and is central to the ways in which you develop and think as a teacher. It is probably the case that on the whole you have acquired your subject knowledge for purposes other than teaching. You are now faced with several questions about your subject knowledge:

- Is my subject knowledge at this stage very much that of a postgraduate?
- How do I hold this knowledge – as a teacher, or as a learner?
- Through what alternative perspectives might I need to look again at what I know in order to teach pupils?

Your subject knowledge can be divided into different kinds of knowledge, understanding and skills. If you attempted to divide your knowledge up in a schematic way, you might end up with something like this:

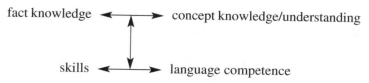

In other words, everything is linked to and depends on everything else. Try to tease out these components not only in relation to your own subject knowledge, but in relation to what you want your pupils to learn.

You might have already experienced the difficulty of finding an appropriate level at which to begin the teaching of a specific National Curriculum requirement for your subject. You might have found yourself talking above the heads of your pupils by:

- using unfamiliar vocabulary;
- making erroneous assumptions about what pupils already know and understand;
- attempting to convey the conceptual content of the lesson by talking at pupils instead of engaging them in their own explorations and discussions;
- not realizing that you need to break down the content you wish to teach into a series of small steps to lead to your pupils' confident grasp of the whole;
- not yet knowing how to break down the content.

Whatever your current subject knowledge, you will obviously recognize your responsibility in enhancing it through reading and study, and you are encouraged to maintain this approach to all your teaching throughout your career. The better informed you are across the widest possible area, the more you will be able to help your pupils.

SUMMARY

- consider the National Curriculum for your subject from a critical perspective;
- recognize the skills pupils need to be taught across the curriculum and talk with colleagues about how they teach them;
- consider what your subject knowledge base is at this stage.
- decide what you will still need to learn;
- work out how knowledge, skills, language and conceptual understanding link together to constitute your subject knowledge.
- reflect on lessons which you have planned at too high a level of understanding for your pupils, and work out ways of changing your approach;
- continue to develop your subject knowledge, and maintain this throughout your career.

STANDARDS

This chapter will support your thinking about issues implicit in the following standards. Trainees:

2.1;   have a secure knowledge and understanding of the subject you are training to teach;

2.1.c;   know and understand relevant National Curriculum programmes of study.

Chapter 5

Literacy across the Curriculum

This chapter offers some advice and information about Literacy across the Curriculum, and about your responsibility to support the development of your pupils' literacy levels. You may not instinctively feel that literacy is within your domain, and may indeed feel quite resistant to the idea that you should take any responsibility for it. You are encouraged to try to think beyond the constraints of your subject area, and of the weight of curriculum which you have the responsibility to teach, to the literacy needs of your pupils and to their subsequent opportunities in life beyond school. You should read this chapter in conjunction with the section on 'Language needs' in Chapter 3, and with Chapter 9.

The extensive research conducted on language and learning during the last 40 or so years makes very clear the centrality of language in learning, and the consequent challenge to schools to recognize this and work with it.[1] The government's stated purpose to 'raise standards' resulted in the establishment of the National Literacy Strategy[2] as one component of the so-called National Strategy for Key Stage 3. This purpose was partly generated by the statistics of adult illiteracy in Britain: as many as 20 per cent of adults are judged to be functionally illiterate, meaning that they are likely to have real problems with understanding information which is normally presented as text, and real difficulties in writing beyond the very simplest messages. Such adults have little or no access to well-paid employment, are effectively disenfranchised, and are disproportionately represented in the prison population.[3] There are undoubtedly all sorts of reasons for this situation, but the part played by schools in contributing to it must be acknowledged.

The Literacy Strategy and its adjunct, Literacy across the Curriculum, were finally formulated as a result of pilot studies of literacy materials and approaches. As a result of the findings and recommendations, a comprehensive file of materials and methods was sent to all schools to enable them to train their teachers in approaches to developing literacy through subject teaching. The underlying assumption was that teachers would recognize and accept their part in developing their pupils' literacy. As with previous initiatives aimed at getting all teachers to grasp their responsibility for the language and literacy development of their pupils across subject areas,[4] Literacy across the Curriculum has only been partially successful.

As all teaching is necessarily conducted through language, and as the language backgrounds and experiences of pupils vary considerably, it seems to be fairly obvious that you should have some understanding of how your use of and assumptions about language within your subject teaching affect the learning opportunities of your pupils. It is vital that you do not take pupils' language skills and levels of understanding for granted. Even where a class as a whole *appears* to have understood the content and aims of the lesson, it is highly likely that several individuals will not have actually understood at the level you hoped for. Making assumptions about pupils' language is therefore ill-advised. This means that you do have to be prepared to spend some time ascertaining what your pupils can do and understand, and what you will need to *teach* them in order that they can engage in your lessons, and use and understand language in the ways you expect.

Literacy[5] as a term is, of course, open to a range of interpretation, from the very simple 'being able to read and write' to the much wider and challenging 'critical literacy', an approach which seeks to empower the individual to understand how the different literacies deployed in all textual production (including non-printed texts) constrain and shape possible responses and engagement. A set of definitions which you might find useful, particularly if your subject is not English, is as follows.

By the end of the period of statutory schooling, a literate student can be regarded as one who:

- can read a range of different texts with understanding and for meaning, including non-linguistic texts (graphs, maps, etc.) and non-print texts (film, TV programmes, computer games, etc.);
- can reproduce with confidence examples of similar texts;
- can understand that textual production varies according to audience and purpose;
- can undertake independent study involving response to a range of texts;
- has a critical vocabulary with which to analyse texts met both in the school environment and outside it.

More detailed discussion of the implications of each item in the list above is now given.

Can read a range of different texts with understanding and for meaning, including non-linguistic texts

You will want, and expect, your pupils to be able to read with understanding all the textual materials you use during your teaching, and you will naturally have some ideas about how you might differentiate those materials. You will therefore need to ensure that pupils can read these texts with understanding. This implies that you will need to develop your understanding of how texts work to convey meaning, including knowing that their structure, style, layout and vocabulary have been selected according to genre, purpose and audience. These features apply in equal measure to all texts you are likely to use.

Can reproduce with confidence examples of similar texts

In most subject areas, pupils are required to produce written evidence of their learning and understanding, sometimes with accompanying illustrative material (graphs, maps, diagrams, sketches and so on). They learn from a range of models (including text and course books and worksheets) what these text types look like, and ideally they will have learned a lot about how to produce them during their primary schooling. However, it cannot be taken for granted that they can reproduce these text types, many of which also require the deployment of specific language and styles. Your responsibility therefore is to ensure that they know how to produce the written and visual requirements of your subject area, and that you know what the component parts of these requirements are. This further also requires you to make no assumptions about what your pupils can do or have already been 'taught'.

With regard to many text types, pupils will have been taught the rules governing chronological writing (narrative, recount, reports, instructions) and non-chronological writing (descriptions, letters, comparisons), and to recognize the differences between examples of these. They will also have been taught the textual features of each of these types, and at primary level will have had some opportunities to show their grasp by reproducing examples of them. However, you cannot take any of this for granted. Before you start teaching a class, it is worth spending some time in listing the kinds of textual production you will be asking of your pupils, and checking that you know how to teach them the requirements for each one.

During Key Stage 3 in geography for example, pupils are required to 'describe', 'describe and explain', 'communicate in different ways', 'identify, describe and explain', 'explore'; all these imply textual production of specific kinds, but within the general context of geographical knowledge and understanding. While it could be argued that when pupils 'describe' in geography they produce a piece of text that shares features with a 'describe' text in history or English, for example, and therefore they 'know' how to describe, nevertheless, the geography teacher does need to know what a 'describe' text in geography looks like. One of the requirements, for example, is that pupils should be taught 'to describe and explain the physical and human features that give rise to the distinctive character of places'. This kind of descriptive writing would obviously look rather different from a descriptive piece in English, for example, written from a different perspective about the same place. For the geography teacher, therefore, it is important to distinguish and recognize the specific features required in such writing, and to ensure that pupils know how to reproduce them. It may be that this requirement can be covered in note form, or using a grid, rather than as a piece of extended writing; however, the more pupils are taught explicitly about text types and how to produce them the better.

These observations apply equally to other subject areas. Success in education for pupils depends as much on pupils' ability to control and manipulate language as on their understanding and knowledge base.

Can understand that textual production varies according to audience and purpose

This ability is connected to the overarching and important consideration that pupils need to be helped during their time in school to develop a critical vocabulary and understanding with which to face the big wide world outside. Part of this understanding is to be derived from opportunities for pupils to talk about the texts they are expected to produce and to respond to. In English, for example, exposure to a wide, though necessarily limited, range of texts is integral to the curriculum as a whole, but it is not a good idea for teachers of other subjects to assume that because of this they do not need to pay any attention to text types themselves.

It is helpful to pupils to have purpose and audience made very explicit for each piece of text they are asked to produce. The purpose may often be to demonstrate that pupils have understood something, or to have a reference for later use of something which they have been learning, or to help them further understand and grasp a new concept or set of information through the rehearsing of it as text. Whatever the purpose, it is important that pupils know what it is, and also that they know who the audience will be, and why. Teachers often *imply* to pupils who the audience will be by saying something like: 'I want you to write a description of a Sikh temple for me, by next Monday'. The 'for me' can be interpreted in several ways, but whatever else it says, it certainly tells pupils that the audience for their work will be the teacher.

It is highly motivating for pupils to be asked to produce text for a much wider range of audience, where this is possible, and certainly for their peers. It is possible to suggest theoretical audiences, for example in asking pupils to write an argument to convince a particular reader of the case for or against something; or in another example to write a letter to a made-up person describing an event from the point of view of another made-up person.

The understanding of purpose and audience in relation to text types allows pupils to both analyse and critique what has already been produced, and to apply that understanding to their own text production.

Can undertake independent study involving response to a range of texts

The desired outcome for pupils as a result of their acquisition of this range of literacy skills is that they should be confident enough in their understanding, and application of strategies and of critical approaches, to be able to undertake sustained independent study of the widest range of texts by the end of their period of statutory schooling at 16+. For many pupils, this will seem a somewhat unrealistic aim, but nevertheless it needs to be borne in mind in all teaching endeavours: English teachers alone cannot carry this responsibility. This range of competences becomes especially important at A level and beyond, and pupils' success at higher levels of study to a marked extent will depend on their confidence in working in an informed and critical way with a wide range of text types.

Before pupils reach these higher levels, and while they are still in your hands, you can play a key role in developing your pupils as autonomous learners by periodically asking them to study independently a short subject-related text of any kind using the critical approaches listed below, and to bring their findings to a lesson for discussion.

Has a critical vocabulary with which to analyse texts met both in the school environment and outside it

A critical vocabulary involves pupils in learning how to avoid taking everything they read at face value. In most subject areas the acquisition of this ability is inherent in National Curriculum requirements and it is worth focusing on three of the key skills mentioned: the ability to *evaluate*, to *interpret* and to *consider evidence*.

Each of these skills implies a reader who can apply a range of critical perspectives to texts, and who has some strategies for interrogating texts. Confident and experienced readers are obviously better placed to develop these skills to the expected levels, but all pupils can be helped to move some way towards being able to apply them. Ability to use these skills implies readers who are already alert to the ways in which texts are produced for certain purposes and audiences, and who can interrogate the text in simple ways:

- Who produced this text and why?
- Who financed the production of this text and why?
- What is the apparent purpose of this text?
- Who is the implied audience for this text?
- What other texts might be compared with this one?
- How can I evaluate the validity and reliability of this text?

It is worth planning for opportunities in lessons where pupils can look at any text in use, and ask the questions above. For example, in a science laboratory, in which there might be diagrams, photographs, posters and information on the walls, these can be deliberately used to introduce pupils to the process of questioning text, by using some or all of the examples above. The exercise can be a starter, intended to introduce pupils to some simple examples of the application of scientific enquiry. Similar exercises can be undertaken in other subject areas; the development of pupils as critical receivers of text can be made an overt part of your teaching, and is particularly important at the very least in alerting pupils to the fact that readers are not obliged to believe everything they read.

RELATIONSHIP BETWEEN LITERACY AND TALK

As has been pointed out already, there is a very strong link between pupils' learning and development, and their participation in planned and guided talk. This also applies to pupils' ability to read and write with confidence and fluency; the rehearsal through talk of ideas, knowledge and opinions allows even very unconfident writers and readers to perform at higher levels. In other words, just as there is a strong relationship between learning and talk, so there is a strong relationship between literacy and talk. In developing pupils' talk within this overall context, consideration should be given to the deliberate and planned development of pupils' spoken accuracy, their use of increasingly sophisticated subject-related vocabulary, and their clarity of expression. High expectations with regard to speaking and listening are at least as important for pupils' development as high expectations relating to their written work.

SUMMARY

In addition to the thinking and consideration implicit in this chapter, you are encouraged to:

- accept your responsibility for the literacy of your pupils;
- ensure that you know something about pupils' levels of language use and understanding before embarking on teaching;
- inform yourself of how to teach the specific reading and writing skills necessary in your subject area;
- devise focused and purposeful ways of developing pupils' articulacy through focused speaking and listening.

STANDARDS

This chapter will help you consider some of the issues implicit in the following standards. Trainees:

1.1;   have high expectations of all pupils;

2.1.c; know and understand the relevant frameworks, methods and expectations set out in the National Strategy for Key Stage 3. All those qualifying to teach a subject at Key Stage 3 know and understand the cross-curricular expectations of the National Curriculum and are familiar with the guidance set out in the National Strategy for Key Stage 3;

3.3.1.c; all those qualifying to teach a subject at Key Stage 3 must be able to use the cross-curricular elements, such as literacy, set out in the National Strategy for Key Stage 3, in their teaching, as appropriate to their specialist subject.

NOTES

1 For example see Britton, J. (1970), *Language and Learning.* London: Allen Lane.

2 National Strategy (2002), 'Literacy across the Curriculum'.

3 Definitions of functional illiteracy vary, but by one measure, the ability to compare and evaluate the information given in two simple passages, about 8 million adults, or roughly 20 per cent of the adult population, would be regarded as functionally illiterate.

4 In 1975 the Department of Education and Science produced *A Language for Life* (London: HMSO). This is the report of a committee set up to consider 'All aspects of teaching the use of English, including reading, writing, and speech' and to make recommendations for improving current practice and monitoring the general level of attainment. The findings of the report (thereafter always referred to simply as 'The Bullock Report' or even 'Bullock' after the name of its chairman) resulted in extensive inservice training, which it was hoped would promote teachers' understanding of how they could implement a *Language across the Curriculum*

policy within schools. The long- and shorter-term results were very disappointing, and clearly demonstrated how hard it was for teachers of subjects other than English to understand such a policy, far less put it into practice. The National Strategy is the most recent attempt to promote such a cross-curricular approach. As it is backed by clear official requirements, and has changed the focus slightly, from *language* to *literacy*, it retains much greater currency, despite not being a fully successful initiative.

5   It can be argued that the dominant position accorded to literacy and being 'literate' within the English education system, and the specific focus via the National Strategy on Literacy across the Curriculum, contributes to a devaluing of the primacy of talk in human interactions, and implies that success of any kind will only come to those who are literate. The effect on many pupils, whose main experience of social intercourse is through talk, can be to deny them any effective points of contact with what faces them in classrooms, particularly where teachers require silence for most of their lessons and pupils are faced with textual demands they cannot meet. Within the wider context of human interactions, talk dominates all forms of discourse; talk is the medium through which most transactions between individuals and groups occur in the first instance. The high status given to being literate can have the effect of disenfranchising, marginalizing and alienating many people from the mainstream of social activity.

Chapter 6

Managing lessons and classrooms

During the course of your training and teaching practice, you will have found the need to learn a great deal about how to manage lessons and your classroom, not simply from the point of view of your pupils' progress and development, but from the purely practical point of view of how to manage all the component parts which go into producing successful lessons. You may also have acquired much of this awareness and knowledge from earlier experiences you have had. In this chapter you are invited to begin to think through, plan for and internalize all the 'teacher behaviours' which you will need in order to run your lessons to achieve maximum learning in your pupils. You may have noticed many of these features already, during your observations of practising teachers. This chapter gives you the opportunity to consider them in a more focused way.

FOLLOWING SET PROCEDURES AND SCHOOL POLICIES

Schools have policies to cover many or all of the following which will impact on your management of your classroom and lessons. Policies which cover aspects of school life outside the classroom are not included here:

- the setting of homework;
- rewards and punishment;
- behaviour modification;
- pupils lining up outside classrooms before lessons;
- pupils standing up when an adult enters the room;
- teachers and pupils greeting each other in a formal way at the start of lessons;
- taking of registers and passing on the information;
- transmission of vital information to teachers in classrooms where there is no Tannoy system;
- response to the fire bell.

It is important that you are familiar with all the policies and procedures which apply at your school, and that you comply with them in a professional manner. Your awareness and application of these policies is crucial for the smooth running of your lessons, and to ensure that you are never taken by surprise. Your demeanour in any situation will act as a cue to your pupils; ensure that you are always able to maintain their appropriate behaviour. You should not regard any of these policies as not applying to you, and need to recognize that the failure of just one member of the staff of a school to carry out school policies undermines their efficacy and the smooth running of the school.

RESOURCE PREPARATION AND PLANNING

The resources you will be selecting and relying on in your teaching, and the ways in which you prepare them will depend on:

- the subject you are teaching and its curriculum requirements;
- the teaching space in which you will be working;
- the availability of other staff to help prepare and manage your resources;
- your access to the photocopier, and the limits placed on your use of it;
- your use of course books or other professionally produced material;
- your use of ICT, including whiteboards and PowerPoint;

- your use of other equipment, including OHPs;
- physical materials required by pupils.

In each case, your preparation will need to be done well in advance, and with a clear idea of the learning which your resources are intended to support. As with all successful teaching, the secret lies in thorough and careful preparation.

STARTS AND ENDS OF LESSONS

It is strongly recommended that you make good use of any observation opportunities you have to see how experienced teachers manage the beginnings and endings of their lessons. The importance of these 'bookends' cannot be overstated. The start of any lesson needs to be used to give pupils the most positive signals about the coming lesson, and about the way in which it will be controlled. You need to be consistent, firm but friendly, and convey an immediate sense of purpose and urgency, to give pupils a sense that it is worth their while to actually come into your room. Starts of lessons fall into two main parts: the physical management of pupils' entry into the classroom, including the management of coats, bags, materials on tables and registers; and the actual beginning of the lesson, the point at which many teachers say: 'Right, today we are going to. . .' or 'Sukhbir, what can you tell me about what we did yesterday?' These starts need to be:

- carefully planned and prepared for, especially if resources are to be used;
- immediately engaging;
- closely linked to what will follow.

Plenary sessions towards the end of lessons, which are being systematically encouraged as part of the three- or four-part lesson approach to teaching, need to be carefully built into the lesson plan, to allow pupils to consider and reflect on what they have just been engaged in. (See Chapter 11 for an exemplar plenary session.) The rather superficial approach to plenary sessions, in which pupils are invited to give yes/no answers to simple questions such as: 'These were our lesson objectives: have we met them?', does not allow for real reflection, and as it is a signal to pupils that the lesson is coming to an end, more often than not results in inattention and impatience to be gone.

Ends of lessons fall into two main areas: bringing the learning to an organized and acknowledged end; and ensuring the orderly departure of pupils from the classroom. Ends of lessons are as important as starts: they confirm the expectations you have of pupils' behaviour and engagement, they allow you to make positive comments as pupils leave the room, and they influence the mood in which pupils go out into the corridor, and possibly into their next lesson with another teacher. They also contribute to pupils' idea of you as their teacher, and to their expectations of you the next time you meet them.

At the actual end of the lesson, attention needs to be paid in an organized and purposeful way to the tidying up of the room and the orderly departure of the pupils. If the classroom is not yours, it is important to ensure that you leave it in a proper state for the next class. Typical procedures for ends of lessons include:

- ensuring all paperwork, books and materials are dealt with appropriately;
- asking all pupils to stand behind their chairs;
- allowing one row of pupils to leave the room at a time.

Orderly departure from the room requires determination and consistent (even if tiring) application of the same procedures and expectations about behaviour every time. Pupils acquire a fine ear for 'the bell' (often when it has not rung) and a fine sense of when a lesson is apparently winding down. Pupils are attuned to the length of lessons, and ensuring that the ending is purposeful and controlled needs *planning* for. After the end of the lesson, you may need to speak to pupils who have previously been told to stay behind for one reason or another. This also needs consciously managing, and building into your lesson plan, as both you and the pupil may have another lesson to get to.

LEARNING PUPILS' NAMES

This might seem to be so obvious that it does not need mentioning. In terms of establishing relationships with your pupils, it is very important; you should attempt to learn all pupils' names within the first two weeks of your time with new classes. There are various ways in which you can do this: name tags, labels, name learning games, greeting pupils individually as they come into the room, using mnemonics, and matching pupils to their names as you go through the register. If for no other reason, you need to know names as quickly as possible in order that you can build supportive relationships with your classes, keep proper records of pupils' attainment and know who these records refer to (particularly important when you are reporting to parents), manage your classes efficiently, encourage the active participation of all your pupils in your lessons and demonstrate that you care about your pupils in a fully professional way. From your own experience you will know the importance that you, and therefore by extension your pupils, attach to being known by name, and therefore to feeling acknowledged as an individual.

ORGANIZATION OF RECORDS AND REGISTERS

Whatever system for registering pupils you encounter in schools, it is worth also establishing your own procedures for keeping records of your transactions with pupils, and of their presence or absence. You should know about the legal requirement to maintain attendance registers, and know that the register is regarded as a legal document. It is important that you know whether pupils have been in your lessons, and also important that you follow up unexplained absences. You need to have a record of whether pupils have handed in homework, whether they have taken home books or other resources, and when and how you have marked written work, or given other assessment grades. In other words, you need to establish from the start of your career workable systems which you will be able to maintain. The high importance now placed on grades and estimated grades for examination purposes means that you must be organized to cope with demands made of you by heads of year and heads of department.

Linked with this is your organization of assessment procedures which you might be using in lessons, for example assessments of speaking, or group work. These need recording in order that they can be fed into subsequent, overall assessments.

THE CLASSROOM/LEARNING SPACE AS A PHYSICAL ENVIRONMENT

You are the person who needs to take responsibility for the efficient, safe and beneficial use of the learning space in which you and your pupils will be working, This means that you need to be entirely familiar with health and safety regulations, particularly as they apply where pupils' physical safety could be at risk, as with PE, design and technology, science and other learning involving physical activity, such as drama. In other curriculum areas, awareness of potential dangers to physical safety is also necessary; even an apparently entirely safe classroom can present hazards in the form of trailing flexes, pupils' bags blocking access within the room, equipment such as OHPs and televisions inadequately secured on trolleys or tables, and unsafe furniture.

In addition, you need to keep a watchful eye on the physical environment of the classroom while a lesson is in progress, ensuring that windows, or other ventilation, are appropriately used, that pupils do not present hazards to themselves, for example by tipping their chairs, or to others by leaving bags in the way, or by other inappropriate behaviour, such as throwing objects across the room.

You may be the main user of a classroom or teaching space, but whether you are or not, you should ensure that any damage to the room is immediately reported to the relevant person (probably the school manager). Such damage might include:

- fraying or unsafe carpet or carpet tiles;
- holes in the walls;
- light switches or sockets coming away from the walls;
- broken windows;
- leaking ceilings or leaking round badly fitting windows;

- lighting which does not work;
- blinds and/or curtains which do not work or are torn;
- doors which do not shut properly;
- hinges which need oiling;
- broken equipment or furniture.

The key point here is that you accept that as a user of any teaching space, it is up to you to ensure its best use, in order that your pupils derive maximum benefit from your lessons. It may appear that pupils do not care about their physical environment, but some recent studies[1] have shown that pupils are adversely affected by poorly maintained teaching areas. If for no other reason, the subliminal message conveyed by such environments is that pupils are unimportant, and teachers also, and that nobody is concerned to make the school an attractive and pleasant place to be.

DISPLAYS

In connection with the above section, it is also useful to consider ways in which you can make your teaching space convey positive messages to the pupils: of their importance, the importance of their learning, your concern that they should be better informed and that their written work can be positively acknowledged. The answer is likely to be through the material you display on the classroom walls, and elsewhere in the room, so that all your pupils have access to it. How to make best use of the material you wish to display and of the space you have available will require you to plan thoughtfully. There are also many key pedagogical points to consider, which might come as a surprise:

- What is the point of displaying pupils' work? When it is on the walls, what do you expect pupils to do with it? Do you wish them to share it? Do you wish them to learn from it? How will you ensure that it is valued, and therefore not vandalized?
- If you intend to make general displays, maybe of materials which could be relevant to all your classes, how long will they be relevant for?

- What do you expect your pupils to do with displays of lists of key words, lists of types of text, posters of historical events or person-alities, posters showing the life cycle of the frog, maps of Britain and the world, *pi* to the 500th decimal place, etc? Will you spend time with pupils in actually looking at your displayed material, and maybe discussing it? Or are you regarding it as a more lively form of wallpaper?

There are also practical points to consider, such as how much time you will attempt to make available to work on your displays, so that you change them regularly, and certainly at least once every half-term. The same display in a room over a year-long period conveys the same message to pupils, and other users, of an ill-maintained teaching space: pupils don't matter, and the teacher cannot be bothered to enliven the teaching space with stimulating and educative materials.

In addition, who will be responsible for actually producing your displays? Will you ever ask pupils to produce displays? If not, where in your room can pupils' presentational work or their feedback as a result of discussions and group/class work be shown?

SUMMARY

You are encouraged during this chapter to undertake a range of actions which will enhance your efficacy as a classroom teacher. Many are self-evident, but these are worth identifying separately:

- in all your planning, ensure that you have taken account of everything included in the chapter;
- ensure that you learn pupils' names as quickly as possible;
- ensure that you keep your own records efficiently;
- keep your displays interesting, relevant and up to date by changing them frequently and being clear about their purpose;
- find out and follow the relevant school policies.

STANDARDS

This chapter will help you think about issues implicit in the following standards. Trainees:

1.5; can contribute to, and share responsibly in, the corporate life of schools;

1.8; are aware of, and work within, the statutory frameworks relating to teachers' responsibilities;

2.5; know how to use ICT effectively, both to teach their subject and to support their wider professional role;

2.7; know a range of strategies to promote good behaviour and establish a purposeful learning environment;

1.3; select and prepare resources, and plan for their safe and effective organization, taking account of pupils' interests and their language and cultural backgrounds, with the help of support staff where appropriate;

3.2.6; record pupils' progress and achievements systematically to provide evidence of the range of their work, progress and attainment over time;

3.2.7; are able to use records as a basis for reporting on pupils' attainment and progress orally and in writing, concisely, informatively and accurately for parents, carers, other professionals and pupils;

3.3.8; organize and manage the physical teaching space, tools, materials, texts and other resources safely and effectively with the help of support staff where appropriate.

NOTE

1 Studies reported recently in *The Times Educational Supplement* confirmed that pupils react critically to their environment, as do the rest of us. When invited to suggest ways in which their schools could be improved, pupils came up with a surprisingly wide range of sophisticated suggestions, notably the improvement of toilet facilities. They also indicated that poorly maintained classrooms had a negative effect on their attitudes and gave them low expectations of the lessons held in them.

Chapter 7

Managing learning

This chapter encourages you to think carefully about what will be going on in your classroom from the point of view of your pupils as learners, and suggests a range of methods which will maintain pupils' engagement throughout your lessons. The underpinning pedagogy of these methods is not given here, though some of it can be deduced easily enough. For a more theorized treatment of pedagogy, refer to Appendix 1. The chapter is divided into two sections: the first is focused on more general methods, which can be applied in any teaching situation; the second is focused more specifically on fundamental methods of managing learning, and on the organization this entails.

GENERAL METHODS

Challenges

It might be assumed that all lessons include some kind of challenge for pupils, if only in the new learning that they are being faced with. However, it is clear from Ofsted and other evidence that lessons often do not include challenges of the desired kind, and in some instances pupils are merely faced with the challenge of colouring in pictures, or copying out of books or off the whiteboard. Real challenge, which fully engages pupils' minds in a variety of ways, needs to be carefully thought about, and also needs to be included in every lesson. Challenge is implicit in some of the other suggestions being made here, but the following can also help.

Simple challenges

- solve puzzles related to previous lessons – these can be on the whiteboard or on paper;
- taking account of previous lesson, guess what this lesson will be about;
- spring a surprise (another teacher comes in to hold a pre-arranged dialogue with you about the content of the lesson, for example);
- use your starter activity to provide the challenge;
- only allow pupils into your room when they give you the proper password (accept anything which shows they are thinking about your subject, or last lesson maybe).

More fundamental challenges

- make the purpose of the lesson a real challenge, perhaps by suggesting that other groups of pupils have found it difficult, but you are convinced that this class will manage it;
- include a lot of thinking in the lesson – emphasize to pupils that you are looking for their best ideas and thoughts;
- include a lot of talk in the lesson, and challenge pupils to show how well they can listen to each other, and how well they can contribute in class;
- challenge the pupils to be ready to tell you at the end of the lesson a specified number of things that they have learned.

Above all, keep up the pace and the energy levels of the lesson. You need to show pupils that you have consistently high expectations of their levels of achievement, and their concentration, and that you are totally committed to their progress.

Pupils at the front of the class

Pupils tend to listen to each other with a great deal more attention than they often listen to teachers, so one way of exploiting the results of speaking and listening work, and any other work, is to have pupils at the front actually *teaching* the rest of the class. This could involve explaining new understanding, showing how a particular answer has been reached, actually teaching something new or describing how a particular problem was solved and the thinking processes involved.

Obviously, there are many more possible uses of this approach. The pedagogical advantages will depend to a large extent on how you set up this approach in the first place. The main ones are that pupils are themselves challenging each other, they are consolidating their learning in going through the process of teaching it, and they are gaining the confidence to stand in front of others and talk with a real educative purpose.

The rather more common teacher practice of having pupils out at the front to show what they have done is less useful. While it undoubtedly serves the purpose of 'celebrating' what pupils have achieved, it is less clear what its educational value is. A very real problem with this practice is what the rest of the class is expected to be doing while individuals or groups show or explain their work. If this is a method you would wish to use, you do need to plan carefully to allow the rest of the class to be engaged in meaningful responses to what they are observing, and to be conscious of how boring this can be for pupils when they are expected to respond to the tenth version of the same content. Other disadvantages of this practice are the risk of negative reactions from pupils to others' work, which can be very demoralizing, or the risk of bland, undifferentiated praise which does nothing to point the way forward for those who have experienced difficulties.

The essential difference between these two versions of pupils at the front is that in the first pupils are teaching, explaining and ideally getting the rest of the class to respond, whereas in the second pupils are merely showing.

Interesting and purposeful outcomes

Encouraging pupils to aim for a desired outcome is often a very good way of maintaining their commitment during a lesson. It can be even better if the outcome will result in pupils or adults outside the classroom being asked to respond in some way. This is another way of varying the audience for pupils' work. In all subject areas, opportunities can be set up for pupils to share and show with pupils from another class, and with good planning, opportunities can also be set up for another adult (teacher, head of department, head of year, headteacher, parent) to be involved in responding to pupils' achievement.

Outcomes for many lessons may not seem particularly riveting: 'Finish Exercise 25', 'Write up your experiment results, for homework if necessary', 'Make sure you have finished your writing by the end of the lesson' and so on. In all instances, with thoughtful planning, outcomes can be made much more useful, purposeful and clearly linked to all pupils' learning. The use of planned plenary sessions can help contribute to this where appropriate. The example given in the section above of pupils showing their work can also be regarded as a motivating outcome, even if it does not always work as the greatest show on earth.

An example from English of an outcome which successfully engaged a whole class involved pupils in writing a letter of thanks to the local mayor after they had visited his rooms in the town hall. Each pupil wrote a letter, after due discussion of what needed to be in it. Pupils then read each other's letters in small groups and each group chose the one they thought best. These best letters were then read out to the whole class, who were asked to vote for the one they preferred. This letter was then typed up properly, shown to the class, and then sent to the mayor. The letter sent by the mayor in reply was shown and read out to the class. All pupils in the class felt that they had been involved in this, and felt particularly pleased that the mayor had actually written to them. This little exercise consolidated pupils' learning about letter writing, confirmed that letters occur in the 'real' world and that they produce responses, and developed a range of skills: collaborative group work, evaluation in judging letters and turn-taking in voting.

Range of activities

To keep up pupils' attention and motivation for the hour which is the length of many lessons, it is often useful to vary the activities you are asking them to engage in. In most subject areas, teachers will automatically plan for a range of activities, but it can be the case that pupils may only be involved in one or two different kinds of activity. For your subject area, think about the possible ranges of appropriate activities (several have been suggested at various points in this book) and consider the validity of each of them, and what benefits for pupils will occur if you use any of them. You do need to be careful not to overload pupils with too many different things they must do, and you do also have to be aware of how you are going to manage the transition from one activity to the next, particularly if pupils have not finished.

It is not a good idea to vary activities for the sake of it, but it is a good idea to use a carefully chosen set of activities which will help pupils to progress. Similarly, it is not a good idea to use activities simply for the sake of keeping pupils occupied; activities must have a logical place in the learning continuum you are setting up in your lesson. As mentioned earlier, it is also important to consider the kind of concentration which activities make possible, and to avoid using so many activities that the development of pupils' attention spans is seriously disrupted.

As with much else that has been suggested, talking with your pupils about how they react to multiple activities and what their thoughts are about their use in lessons will help you in your future planning.

Rewards

It is perhaps an indictment of the English education system that in order to motivate pupils to want to learn, there are occasions when teachers resort to bribery in order to keep pupils on task over extended periods. The interesting thing about this is that the bribery often works well to begin with, but because it has actually helped pupils become engaged in ways they had not been before, they find the work itself its own reward after a time, and cease to be interested in bribes. Naturally, the nature of the bribe is important here; sweets are a common one, and do cease to be motivating quite quickly. More ambitious bribes, operating over a longer time span, such as pupils being taken out of school for trips or visits of various kinds once they have completed several weeks' work, are also sometimes used by teachers and schools. Other kinds of reward, such as school, house or year points, merits, book tokens or other payments for achieving a certain number of points or merits, are also used by schools as a whole, and operate as a more subtle form of bribery.

Taking account of different times of day and different times of the week

As experienced teachers know, pupils can vary quite markedly in their behaviour and their ability to concentrate according to the time of day and the day of the week. Rather than fighting against this tendency, it is worth considering how to work with it in your planning of lessons. Characteristically, the worst times of the week are afternoons, and Friday afternoons are, of course, renowned for being the most difficult. It is sensible, therefore, to attempt to use lessons in which pupils are likely to be more amenable for more challenging work, and to make more difficult times of the week enjoyable in other ways. It should be noted, however, that with proper lesson planning, management strategies and an understanding of how to motivate pupils, even Friday afternoon lessons can be highly successful.

It is not recommended that you attempt to take the easy way out, and give pupils non-educative work to do at difficult times of the week. Whatever you plan for, you should continue to aim high, to maintain high expectations, and to emphasize to your pupils the seriousness and importance of what you are all engaged in.

FUNDAMENTAL METHODOLOGY

Use of active approaches

Active approaches place pupils in learning situations where they are doing more of the thinking and exploration inherent in the lesson than is possible for most pupils when a more passive, transmissive method is employed by the teacher. In order to help pupils become actively engaged, a range of methodology has to be employed, of which some examples are given here. The role of the teacher in all these situations is of crucial importance, and needs to be carefully planned for. It is not a good use of precious lesson time to undertake any of these methods without first having thought through very carefully what you expect them to achieve for your pupils' learning, how you will set them up and how you will ensure that your intended outcomes will be attained.

Pair work

The advantages of pair work over other kinds of organization are:

- pupils are more likely to remain on task;
- the teacher can pair up pupils for maximum learning potential;
- there is less likelihood of noise levels becoming unacceptable;
- each pupil is given more opportunity to speak, exchange and share, and attain new learning;
- feedback from pair work can be arranged to occur within bigger groupings;
- feedback is fairer and gives more pupils opportunities to speak.

Where the lesson plan involves pupils in discussion, or exploration, pair work is more likely to allow less confident pupils to make a contribution, as they are not being exposed to the whole class, and one-to-one discussion can boost confidence. You are recommended to experiment with pair work, in order to find the best ways of using it, and the feedback from it.

The disadvantage of pair work is that it depends, as do most other methods of arranging pupils, on pupils being willing to engage in it in a purposeful manner. To prevent pupils from simply using the time for off-task chat, you need to ensure that you use tight time limits, and that pupils are convinced of the purpose of the work. As with group work, pair work needs to be set up clearly, and depending on what it entails, pupils may need coaching in how to do it.

Group work

Advantages of group work are:

- unconfident pupils can find their feet without being discouraged by being put on the spot;
- more ideas are available to the group as a whole;
- discussion and exploration can be undertaken at greater depth;
- where the teacher has organized group work by using roles within the groups, pupils can experience a variety of roles during the course of a year; for example, chairperson, scribe, speaking for an idea, speaking against an idea, or, as is possible in many subject areas, taking on roles within exploratory scenarios;
- the teacher can move around from group to group during the session more easily than from pair to pair, gaining some idea of individual pupils' thinking and performance.

It is clear, however, that group work requires as much overt organization as any other form of classroom organization. Pupils generally need to be trained in the art of participating in such learning, and certainly always require a set of operational rules and understandings. You will need to consider the following if you decide that group work is going to achieve optimal learning outcomes for your pupils:

- the best number for groups; four or five should be a maximum, depending on what the pupils are being expected to do;
- which pupils you will group together; it is rarely a good idea to allow friendship groups to become learning groups, as the temptation to go off task is great. It is preferable to mix pupils in groups according to their strengths and needs, so that lower achieving pupils are placed with higher achieving pupils;

- how the roles within groups are to be allocated;
- how the work will be organized;
- what kind of results you are expecting from group work and how these are to be shared;
- what you intend to happen to the work pupils have done: will it be seen to be of value by the pupils so that they can feel that it was a worthwhile exercise and not just an excuse to chat?

The disadvantages of group work that has not been set up properly are: pupils rarely, if ever, stay on task; a few more responsible pupils do all the work, while the others sit back, chat and generally behave inappropriately; the focus of the lesson is lost; you have the problem of deciding how you are going to manage the feedback – it can become very tedious for pupils to listen to the findings of other groups, especially if all groups were set exactly the same exercise; and if groups do come up with something acceptable, you have no means of knowing who produced it, which means that you cannot adequately assess pupils for their understanding and development.

Speaking and listening

In spite of the greater emphasis now being placed on speaking and listening in several areas of the curriculum, some of this via the practices of assessment for learning, it is very often the case that teachers prefer pupils to be quiet during lessons. The findings of research conducted during the 1960s and 1970s which showed the primacy of speaking and listening in pupils' learning, and which even coined the term 'oracy'[1] as an equivalent to 'literacy', have gradually been sidelined in the official literature. Although the research did eventually lead to the inclusion of speaking and listening in the National Curriculum, the way in which this was done contributed to an impression that speaking and listening could be regarded as an extra, a bolt-on to the main business of the classroom. This does not mean that pupils are silent in lessons; indeed, many teachers tolerate low levels of chat and noise. What it does mean is that the learning possibilities offered by structured, well-grounded oral interactions within whole classes are often little understood, and even less frequently consciously planned for.

As well as the obvious oral interactions which take place within pair and group work, it is important that you consider how you can use speaking and listening in an active way as you conduct whole class learning, exploration and investigation. Initially, therefore, it is a good idea to honestly assess what happens to pupils' learning when the teacher conducts 'discussions' (and indeed what the word 'discussion' actually means in this context), or question-and-answer sessions, where all the offerings of pupils are directed at the teacher only. A diagram of such interactions would show a linear pattern with the teacher as the recipient of converging lines, rather like the diagrams of shots at goal in a football match. Consideration of this might allow you to see that this practice emphasizes the authority of the teacher, diminishes the importance of what pupils are offering, does not encourage pupils to listen to each other, and does nothing to ensure that *all* pupils in the class have grasped what is being talked about. It also, damagingly, can often place the emphasis on *right* and *wrong*, as this kind of interaction can often place pupils in the position of guessing what the teacher already knows, and frequently only involves a few pupils. It is obvious that it is impossible to conduct an all-inclusive discussion with a class of 25 or more pupils.

A more inclusive practice, involving pupils in sharing their thoughts with each other within the whole class, allows all pupils to be engaged, reduces the dominant role of the teacher, who becomes more of an enabler, and develops the thinking and questioning of pupils. This alternative approach would produce a diagram showing lines of interaction circling round the class, with the teacher only one part of the pattern. How to set up this kind of active speaking and listening? The outlines below should help you, as will further reading of assessment for learning materials and suggestions.

The procedure can be carried out in several ways, but the key strategy is always the same: to use a form of question or suggestion which will open up rather than close down discussion, and an expectation that pupils, not the teacher, will pick up and comment on each other's offerings. The start of the process should also include giving pupils at least a minute of thinking time, so that what is said has at least been considered. When thinking time is over, the teacher asks a pupil to offer their thoughts on the matter in hand, and then asks for other pupils' responses to the first pupil. What gradually develops in the class is a chain of response, which is kept going by the teacher varying the questions from time to time, and also summing up what has been said so that pupils can further develop their thinking and understanding, before the teacher redirects the questions.

As with other teaching approaches covered in this section, this one requires planning and practice. To begin with, it can take time to alter questioning techniques, so that open and not closed questions are asked. Closed questions, of course, close down options for response, and tend to require only one kind of answer; as the pupils know that the teacher already knows the answer, they often cannot see the point of answering. This alternative technique places the emphasis on what the pupils actually think, and allows the teacher to draw out and develop this thinking so that all pupils understand the matter in hand at the end of the session. This pedagogy is used extensively in other education systems, where it can also involve pupils in not only saying what they think, but demonstrating it on the board. Other pupils are then encouraged to show different understanding or interpretation by also showing it on the board, so that pupils also become used to being at the front of the room, and explaining their ideas to the whole class. This places the emphasis very much on the joint learning and exploration of concepts and ideas, and encourages cooperation and collaboration. With this method, mistakes are welcomed as ways of helping learning, rather than seen as 'wrong answers'.

In using these approaches, you need to be very conscious of the kinds of learning you are wanting to support: factual learning, concept development, imaginative exploration, recapitulation and reconsideration, finding out the pupils' starting point, sharing ideas about how learning can be enhanced, are, among others, some of the aims you will have across a range of lessons with your pupils. Selecting the appropriate approach is therefore important.

The following extract describes what typically happens in class-rooms from pupils' perspectives where speaking and listening are not developed as pedagogically central to the teacher's perception of pupils' learning:

- Listen to the teacher, often for long periods at a time
- When the teacher stops talking, bid properly for the right turn to speak yourself, sometimes when competition for the next turn means balancing the risks of not being noticed against the risks of being ignored as too enthusiastic
- Answer questions to which the answer will be judged more or less relevant, useful and correct by a teacher who is seeking not to know something but to know if you know something
- Put up with having anyone's answer treated as evidence of a common understanding or misunderstanding, so that the teacher will often explain something again when you understood it the first time, or rush on when you are still struggling with what was said before
- Look for clues as to what a right answer might be from the way a teacher leads into a question, and evaluates the responses
- Ask questions about the administration of the lesson but not usually about its content (and certainly never suggest that the teacher may be wrong)
- Accept that what you know already about the topic of the lesson is unlikely to be asked for, or to be accepted as relevant, unless and until it fits into the teacher's frame of reference.[2]

You are encouraged to compare this account with your own experiences as a pupil, what you have observed in school and your own practice so far with regard to questioning, and to consider what you should do in order to use such interchanges to promote actual learning.

Drama

Drama which uses role-play and improvised explorations of situations, experiences and concepts can contribute a great deal to pupils' learning in many curriculum areas.[3] You do not need to be a trained drama teacher in order to use drama techniques in your teaching. Many of the most appropriate classroom drama techniques are quite simple to apply, once you have the confidence to allow pupils out of their seats, or to rearrange your classroom. It is useful to remember that this kind of classroom drama is not concerned with performance per se, though presentations might be the end result, but is concerned with setting up active and participatory classroom situations, which will allow all pupils to gain from the experience in a positive way.

Some simple techniques to use, without much change needed in the layout of the classroom, are:

- develop pair work into improvised role-play situations to explore arguments for and against when working on issues which have moral and social implications: for example, one pupil takes on the role of a medieval peasant, the other the role of the feudal lord, in talking about the payment of tithes; or, one pupil takes on the role of a householder and the other a road builder in talking about the compulsory purchase of land for a new road;
- develop group work on the same lines, with the relevant number of roles planned beforehand: for example, in further exploration of a poem about a girl leaving home, pupils take relevant roles in order to hold a case conference about her, with one pupil acting as chair;
- working with the whole class, set up hotseating exercises, in which those in the hot seat are at the front of the classroom, and the rest of the pupils ask them questions about the issue at hand (for greatest learning this requires careful preparation by the pupils);
- use cards appropriately prepared, for example, to allow pupils to explore how word order can be understood and varied in the formation of English sentences, where each pupil is given only one word and contributes by coming to the front to stand in the appropriate place. This exercise in placing words, ideas or even pictures in appropriate sequences can be adapted for use across the curriculum;
- presentations, such as newscasts, where the presenting pupils are at the front, and the rest sitting as an audience.

Techniques involving a change in the layout of the classroom include:

- circle work[4]: the advantages of all the pupils and the teacher sitting in a circle are that the teacher is on the same level as the pupils, and everyone can see everyone else, without opportunities for hiding behind others. There are many ways in which to use a circle layout, all of which develop the cohesiveness of the class, and support the development of respect for each other, of listening skills and readiness, and of confidence in speaking in front of peers. At the very least, the circle layout is conducive to open-ended exploration, and the sharing of thoughts;
- rearranging the room for some kinds of group work, including simulations, where, for example, pupils are placed in the position of editors in a newsroom, deciding which incoming items of news should be broadcast, and making choices of priorities.

In all drama-based work, as with everything else, it is most important that rules have been worked out and agreed beforehand to maximize engagement and learning. Pupils' self-discipline is of key importance at all times, and well-planned, well-prepared drama work can help them achieve this, in addition to the specific learning objectives of the lesson. It is also very important that this work is highly structured and controlled; it is pointless putting pupils in situations like this if they are substantially left to their own devices, with the odd time limit.

Assessment for Learning

Assessment for Learning is included in this section because your application of the techniques suggested, and your understanding of what it means in terms of your pupils' learning, are integral to your pedagogical approach. Assessment for Learning implies a pedagogy based on an understanding of how pupils learn and an understanding of how teachers can bring about that learning.

The current Assessment for Learning theories and research which are being extensively drawn on in a wide range of educational contexts are both grounded in and lead to particular pedagogical understandings. Assessment for Learning research[5] has been concerned with ways in which formative, ongoing assessment can be developed in classroom practices, supported by summative assessment, in order to maximise pupils' learning and achievement. The theoretical underpinning here is the understanding of learning as a recursive process, in which frequent feedback is necessary in order to log what has been achieved and understood, and to propose what is still to be grasped and undertaken.

Recently published National Strategy[6] advice and methodology is based on many of the findings of this research, and emphasizes how the application of the four main ideas about formative assessment can be applied in classrooms. The four ideas are:

- questioning;
- feedback;
- sharing criteria;
- self-assessment.

Questioning

Something has been said about this already, in the section above on speaking and listening. The general positive applicability of the research findings[7] was shown by the responses of the teachers involved, who discovered across a range of subject areas that where questioning became more open, where thinking time was given, and pupils were encouraged to share and question each other's ideas:

- answers were longer;
- failure to respond decreased;
- responses were more confident;
- pupils challenged and/or improved the answers of other pupils;
- more alternative explanations were offered.

Because questioning has such a central role in the ways in which teachers interact with their pupils, it is important that you give time to the consideration of your own approaches to questioning, and that you honestly evaluate the involvement of all your pupils in their learning during your lessons. You will probably find that application of the questioning techniques described above will produce more motivated and engaged pupils.

Additional ways of thinking about your use of questioning are provided by the classification of question types produced by Benjamin Bloom and his colleagues.[8]

Feedback

Pupils need feedback as a continuous way of evaluating how they are performing and learning. It is therefore important that it is included as a matter of course in all lessons, and that both you and your pupils understand its purpose and effect. Oral feedback during lessons is vital, but so is the written feedback in response to pupils' written work. Oral feedback given to pupils during lessons can be much more probing and pedagogically thought through than the very common 'good', 'well done', 'you have all behaved very well this lesson'; indeed, it is important that it should be so. Written feedback similarly needs to be focused on learning and development, and needs to be real feedback, rather than very common comments such as 'good', 'you have done well', 'do this again, it is not acceptable' and so on. All feedback should focus on how pupils are learning, rather than on how they are behaving. Both formative and summative feedback are discussed in greater detail in Chapter 12.

Sharing criteria

Sharing criteria indicates that you are ready to work with your pupils to arrive at commonly agreed ways by which to evaluate the learning achieved in the lesson, as well as ways of questioning and pursuing this further where understanding has not been achieved. This approach runs counter to the prevalent pressure to 'cover' the syllabus, as it acknowledges that not all pupils will learn at the same speed, and allows time for further work. It might include agreements with pupils that those who have understood will help those who have not, and will also ensure that further time is made available for further explanations and exemplification. Another important strand of such an agreement is the undertaking to ensure that pupils understand, and to give them the confidence to speak out when they have not.

Sharing criteria can also include the use of peer assessment, which will enable pupils to help each other through considered application of the agreed criteria to each other's work. It is always very helpful to pupils to know the method and purpose of any assessment before they embark on the lesson; this gives them further information about their learning aims, and contributes to their understanding of the wider context in which they are working.

Self-assessment

This approach to pupils' learning depends on their agreement with and understanding of the shared criteria, and their ability to apply them to their own work. As with all the methods included in assessment for learning, this one helps pupils become much more autonomous, and therefore reduces their dependence on the approval of the class teacher, and allows them to disengage from the *right/wrong* attitude to their learning. It also helps pupils think of what they are engaged in in the classroom as leading to learning, rather than as *work*. The *work* approach on the part of many pupils is worth investigating; it is a learned approach, taught by the way in which teachers talk about what they want pupils to do, for example, 'Jason, get on with your work', where Jason is being encouraged to see what he is being asked to do as somehow disengaged from himself and his sense of his own learning. When he has done his *work*, he will give it in, and it may or may not be marked, and he may or may not ever hear anything about it again. Consideration of what teachers mean by 'work', and why this word is used about what is going on in classrooms, can lead to some very useful pointers for you about how you want to go about developing pupils as learners.

Using ongoing assessment in lessons

This is included in this chapter because assessment should be one of your means of evaluating how well your lesson has been understood, and how you might need to rethink subsequent lessons in order to ensure that all your pupils have learnt what you set out to teach. At this point, assessment needs to be thought about in the context of your planning, so that you know in advance how you will evaluate each pupil's learning and understanding during the lesson itself.

You are likely to make quick assessments of your pupils' learning by observing how they perform and react, and by looking at written work they may be involved in. In other words, you will be developing ways of making quick, informal assessments as the lesson proceeds. It is advisable to have predicted problems that might occur, and to have planned what you will do should they do so. Your ability to interpret the reasons for problems arising will to a large extent dictate the appropriateness of your response. It is not helpful to your development as a successful teacher to ascribe problems in lessons simply to pupils' misbehaviour. Their misbehaviour has a cause, and it is highly likely to be to do with the way in which you have set up and conducted the lesson, unpalatable though this may be to accept. You need, therefore, to be able to assess your own performance as well as the pupils'.

If your ongoing assessment tells you that some pupils have not grasped the learning intentions of the lesson, you will need to have some means of working out why this was so. Did you set the lesson up inappropriately? Did the pupils concerned miss a previous lesson? (In which case, did you manage to do anything about it?) Did you 'get off on the wrong foot' with the class from the start of the lesson? Do you know how to backtrack and start again? Will 'going round' the class and explaining to individual pupils help?

If you decide that you can only retrieve the situation by going over the same material in the next lesson, you will still need to consider what you can learn from this lesson about how to make what you are teaching accessible to your pupils. To this extent, therefore, your assessments have to be considered, careful, realistic, looking as much at your own performance as at the pupils', and above all have to be planned in as part of your lesson.

SUMMARY

The suggestions made in this chapter are self-explanatory. You are recommended to consult the references given to extend your understanding of assessment for learning and the range of classroom methods described. Appendix 4 gives an outline of a programme for teaching effectively based on the results of a research project. This is the Teacher Effectiveness Enhancement Programme.

STANDARDS

This chapter will help you think about some of the issues implicit in the following standards. Trainees:

1.2; treat pupils consistently, with respect and consideration, and are concerned for their development as learners;

1.3; demonstrate and promote the positive values, attitudes and behaviour that they expect from their pupils;

2.4; understand how pupils' learning can be affected by their physical, intellectual, linguistic, social, cultural and emotional development;

2.7; know a range of strategies to promote good behaviour and establish a purposeful learning environment;

3.1.1; set challenging teaching and learning objectives which are relevant to all pupils in their classes;

3.3.3; teach clearly structured lessons or sequences of work which interest and motivate pupils and which: make learning objectives clear to pupils; employ interactive teaching methods and collaborative group work; promote active and independent learning that enables pupils to think for themselves and to plan and manage their own learning;

3.3.7; organize and manage teaching and learning time effectively;

3.3.9; set high expectations for pupils' behaviour;

3.3.14; recognize and respond effectively to equal opportunities issues as they arise in the classroom.

NOTES

1 See Wilkinson, A. (1990), 'Introduction: the concept of oracy – retrospect and prospect', in Wilkinson, A., Davies, A. and Berrill, D., *Spoken English Illuminated*. Buckingham: Open University Press. Wilkinson gives the following account: '"The spoken language in England has been shamefully neglected." This was the opening sentence of the original edition of *Spoken English* (Wilkinson 1965, with Davies and Atkinson). At that time reading and writing (literacy) dominated the curriculum, both as a means of learning and a method of discipline. A parallel term was needed to give equivalent status to talking and listening, hence "oracy" was offered.'

2 Edwards, A. D. (1992), 'Teacher talk and pupil competence', in K. Norman (ed.), Thinking Voices: The work of the National Oracy Project. London: Hodder and Stoughton. Quoted in Alexander, R. (2000), Culture and Pedagogy. Oxford: Blackwell Publishing Ltd.

3 Hodgson, J. (ed.) (1972), *The Uses of Drama*. London: Methuen.

4 For more on this see http://www.teachernet.gov.uk/teachingand learning/library/circletime/

5 Black, P., Harrison, C., Lee, C., Marshall, B. and William, D. (2003), *Assessment for Learning*. Maidenhead: Open University Press.

6 Key Stage 3 National Strategy (2004), *Assessment for Learning: Guidance for senior leaders*. London: HMSO.

7 See Black, P. *et al. op. cit.* Teachers' work on this project forms the research focus of this book, and their responses to the approaches being trialled are informative and perceptive.

8 Bloom, B. S. (1956), *Taxonomy of Educational Objectives*: *The classification of educational goals. Handbook 1: Cognitive domain.* New York: Longmans, Green. For a schematic version see www. officeport.com/edu/blooms.htm

Chapter 8

Managing behaviour

This chapter is concerned with helping you develop your understanding of how to manage pupils' behaviour in your classroom. For some teachers in schools where there is weak senior management direction and control, and where disciplinary procedures are inconsistently carried out, managing behaviour in the classroom can be made much more difficult. It is always better to work with others in your department if at all possible, in sharing experiences and strategies, and in offering and receiving support.

UNDERSTANDING AND ABIDING BY OVERALL SCHOOL POLICIES AND PRACTICE

Reference has already been made to some of these in the last chapter. They are revisited here in order that you recognize the importance of:

- knowing school policies and practice;
- knowing who to ask for help and advice;
- taking advantage of all training opportunities offered to you to learn more about behaviour management;
- seeking out and reading some of the currently available material dealing with behaviour management.

UNDERSTANDING PUPILS' BEHAVIOUR

This section is concerned with the behaviour pupils exhibit in your classroom which could be regarded as closely tied in with your management of the lesson. The wider implications of understanding pupils' behaviour, such as the effect on them of poor nutrition, home circumstances and parental attitudes, behavioural disorders such as the so-called attention deficit behavioural disorder (ADBD)[1] and behaviours related to disabilities and diagnosed conditions such as autism, need to be researched by you at greater length than is possible here. For many pupils exhibiting such behaviours, your school SENCO should be able to at least give you some diagnostic information and advice, and for other pupils information may be available from a head of year or a form tutor.

While it will not always be the case that what you do produces the behaviour you observe in your pupils, very often this will be so. The key, therefore, is to recognize how this cause and effect operates, and to ensure that you are able to modify what you do in order to produce desired behaviours.

In general terms, pupils will 'behave' when they:

- feel secure with the way lessons are conducted;
- know what the rules and expectations are, and know that they will be applied consistently;
- are respected by being consulted about rules and expectations, and other aspects of the lesson including assessment;
- are respected for their contributions and ideas;
- believe in the validity of the lesson and can see its benefits to them;
- are encouraged and supported in their efforts;
- recognize that the teacher believes in the importance of what pupils are asked to do;
- recognize that the teacher is interested in developing them as thinkers and learners;
- enjoy a good working relationship with the teacher who behaves professionally and with dignity.

Suggestions are given here of positive and enabling ways of maintaining pupils' readiness to engage with commitment and motivation in your lessons.

HOW TO ADDRESS PUPILS

When pupils meet you for the first time they will be trying to work out what kind of teacher you are and therefore how they will stand in your regard. Their first clue to this will be the words they hear you say, and the tone, volume and authority with which you say them. First impressions are naturally always important, so it will be to your advantage to have worked out in advance, and if necessary rehearsed, how you will address your classes.

Some trainees have already developed what appears to be an innate grasp of what to say and how to say it, and find that addressing pupils appropriately comes naturally to them; others do not find this so easy. Some advice is given here to help you shape a language and style which will support the development of a cooperative, friendly atmosphere in your classroom. Your aim is to foster a positive, engaged and focused learning approach; the language you use will play a crucial part in realizing this aim.

Vocabulary

- Using 'we' more than 'I' and 'you' will immediately convey your collaborative attitude: 'I' signals focus on yourself.
- Phrases like: 'We are going to see/find out/think about/focus on/consider/discuss' rather than 'What I want you to do today is. . .' signal an invitation to pupils to see themselves and their ideas as central to what you are steering them towards.
- Saying 'How could we work on this?' or 'What do we know already about this?' signals your genuine interest in pupils' ideas.
- Asking and negotiating rather than commanding demonstrates that control is not your only aim and also conveys respect.

- Words which denote cooperation and joint engagement in the lesson encourage pupils: help, support, think, ideas, offer, suggest, guess, predict.

Tone and volume

- Keep volume as low as possible: if you have to raise your voice to get attention, lower it again as soon as pupils have quietened.
- Maintain a consistent volume, allied to a friendly tone.
- Avoid talking in 'teacher mode', which consists of a consistently raised voice, sometimes on the verge of shouting; this is not conducive to a learning atmosphere, can be abrasive and is always intrusive.
- Vary tone, pace and volume, especially if you are reading aloud to pupils.
- Demonstrate that you respect your pupils by never shouting (always a sign that you have failed to maintain control).

Modes of address

Do not:

- insult pupils;
- use sarcasm against pupils;
- tease pupils;
- bully pupils;
- threaten pupils;
- seek to prove that you are the 'boss'; they know that already;
- tell pupils what another teacher has told you about them, whether negative or positive;
- say to pupils that you taught their sibling/s and have negative/ positive expectations of the whole family (pupils find this highly embarrassing).

Modes of address

Do:

- speak in a friendly way to all pupils;
- at different points of a lesson, depending on what the pupils are doing, use words of support for the educational/thinking progress they are making;
- maintain through your choice of language a professional, adult and neutral approach.

Signalling transitions

In most lessons what one might call 'throat clearing' moments arise, when the teacher needs to signal some kind of change in direction or activity. Throat clearing words tend to be 'Listen', 'Right', 'OK' or 'Now then', followed by general instructions: 'Put your pens down, face this way and listen to me'; 'When you have finished. . .'; 'You have one minute left to finish. . .' and so on. Whatever you choose to say at these moments, you need to remain conscious of the effect your words will have on your pupils, and ensure that you maintain a neutral stance.

PREPARING WHAT YOU WILL SAY

After the first lessons you teach, consider the points at which you felt that words failed you, and make a note of these. Make notes of the words which teachers you are observing use at specific points of lessons:

- entry into the classroom and very beginning of the lesson;
- transition to a starter;
- words during the starter;
- transition to the first activity;
- words during the activity;
- transition to plenary/end of lesson;
- words at end of lesson.

You could also with benefit listen to and note down all the ways in which teachers:

- address individuals;
- speak to latecomers;
- signal disapproval;
- speak in order to manage giving out and taking in of materials, books, stationery.

Once you have made your notes, you will need to decide whether any of these modes of address will suit you as a teacher, and therefore whether you will use them. Otherwise, you will need to work out a form of words which you find appropriate.

USE OF PRAISE

A very common method of motivating pupils is to praise them, sometimes for the most trivial and poor so-called achievements. The 'theory' behind this very common practice is that pupils need their self-esteem and confidence to be constantly bolstered. There are several problems this gives rise to:

- it becomes very difficult to suggest to pupils how they might improve, as this can be seen as having a negative effect on their sense of self-worth;
- praising pupils often focuses on behaviour rather than learning;
- praising pupils for producing half a page of poorly written work, simply because that is the best that has yet been achieved by them, tends to confirm them in their own underachievement;
- praise confirms the teacher in the role of assessor, rather than encouraging self-assessment by pupils.

Use of praise is, therefore, rather more complex than might at first appear. It does require you to think through why you are using praise at all, and what responses might be more conducive to pupils' progress. In other education systems, praise is not regarded as leading to learning, and forms no part of teachers' pedagogical approaches. Assessment for Learning approaches are more likely to allow you to avoid the use of 'empty' praise, and to help you focus pupils much more rigorously on what they are learning. You are encouraged to give some thought to the ways in which praise is used as you observe teachers at work; in particular, observe how pupils react to praise, and how pupils who have not been praised also react. Observe the circumstances in which praise is used: is it used to support real learning, thinking and engagement, or is it used to encourage certain kinds of behaviour? Consider the extent to which praise produces a competitive atmosphere between pupils, and the extent to which teachers extend unfocused, generalized praise to all pupils in order to appear even-handed.

You are strongly encouraged in your own teaching to find other positive ways of acknowledging pupils' thinking and development rather than using praise: 'That is an interesting/thoughtful/probing/ inspiring answer'; 'Can you add anything to your interesting ideas?'; 'You have thought of a helpful answer; what else do you think we need to find out?'; 'Could you share your idea with the whole class?', and so on.

MOTIVATIONAL TACTICS[2]

Commonly used motivational tactics, which can smack more of threats and punishments than of a real concern that pupils will learn, tend to focus on formal outcomes, such as summative assessments in the form of tests and examinations, or sometimes even warnings about jobs, life after school or admission to further or higher education. There is no doubt that such tactics can work, but only if they are tailored to the specific needs of individual pupils. Pupils' notions of what they will be doing when they leave school have a direct bearing on their attitudes to learning, and some thought needs to be given to how best to use this information as a motivational tool, where possible.

Otherwise, pupils' motivation to apply themselves in the classroom is the result of both intrinsic and extrinsic factors: intrinsic factors tend to be those which pupils bring into the classroom with them, and extrinsic factors tend to be those which the school supplies in various forms. One way of dividing these two is to regard intrinsic motivation as resulting in a desire to learn out of curiosity and for the sake of learning, whereas extrinsic motivation is more likely to be a desire to learn for the sake of some external reward. Most pupils will exhibit a mixture of these two kinds of motivation; it is more common to see intrinsic motivation in younger, pre-secondary pupils, and more common to see extrinsic motivation working with older, secondary pupils. You will need to learn how to recognize these two forms at work, and to use appropriate methods to encourage all your pupils. You will also need to take account of pupils hiding their real interests and motivation to avoid the teasing and disapprobation of their peers. A skilful teacher can work round these undoubtedly powerful negative influences which pupils bring to bear on themselves and each other, but it is more likely that a whole school ethos which supports and rewards achievement is necessary in order for individual teachers to succeed.

In the case of pupils who exhibit weak motivation in applying themselves to learning or doing anything worthwhile for themselves in the classroom, you will find it useful to have a range of motivational tactics at your disposal. Weak motivation can appear to be the result of a very wide range of factors, but the dominant one is probably serious lack of belief in oneself and one's capabilities, and a very weak sense of self-worth. Pupils who fall into this category have probably rarely if ever experienced success at school, and are likely to have fallen so far behind their peers that they have given up completely. Such pupils are also very likely to have behavioural problems, not necessarily the obvious ones, but problems such as low concentration levels, reluctance to participate, a desire to remain unnoticed at the back of the class and lack of social skills. Even very young pupils with such problems are aware of their position, and pre-empt criticism by voicing their own view of their failures: 'I'm no good', 'We're the bottom set, we can't do that', 'I'm useless' and so on.

Motivation of such pupils depends to a very large extent on the teacher's:

- determination and conviction that pupils can be motivated;
- confidence in using a range of teaching approaches which value individual and collaborative effort and contribution;

- selection of appropriate classroom strategies aimed at enabling all pupils to succeed, such as a high priority given to structured talk;
- realistic acceptance of where pupils' strengths might lie, and focusing on these before tackling weaknesses;
- encouragement of pupils to assess themselves, and cooperate in peer assessment.

Motivation of pupils for tests and examinations

Naturally, there is a very wide range of pupil attitudes in this context, and it is worth thinking about how to engage reluctant pupils working towards qualifications. It is important to be aware of the significant challenges which tests and examinations pose to pupils at all levels. It is also important to recognize that just because tests and examinations are important to you and your school, they may well not be important to some of your pupils. Rather than seeing them as the *sine qua non* of their educational achievement, they may very well regard them as irrelevant, boring and alienating. Your job, therefore, is to find ways in which to engage your pupils in the content of the examination specification, and to avoid using the passing of the examination itself as the sole motivator for your pupils.

The challenges to all pupils, and particularly to lower achieving pupils, of tests and examinations, remain the same throughout the period of compulsory schooling, and need to be recognized and acknowledged:

- fear of failure;
- intense worry in the period leading up to the test/examination, resulting in negative physical symptoms, including in worst cases suicidal attitudes;
- difficulty in understanding and learning content;
- difficulty in acquiring and being able to deploy the requisite skills;
- lacking proper opportunities for quiet study;
- unrealistic parental expectations;
- unrealistic teacher expectations;
- pressures to succeed exerted by the school as a whole.

The psychological effect on pupils of being barred from tests and examinations in case their low grades negatively affect a school's examination status and league table position also needs to be considered. The whole apparatus of testing and examining is unquestioningly accepted by most schools and for many teachers becomes the *raison d'être* of all their work. Pupils are not consulted about this aspect of their Key Stage 4 curriculum, other than making choices of subjects for study.

CONVEYING RESPECT

Your attitudes to your pupils will be clear to them very quickly. Given the teacher-dominated mode of most teaching and classroom inter-action, pupils are highly sensitized to what they think teachers think of them, and can react adversely where they feel patronized, made little of or made the butt of sarcasm. Pupils also feel particularly vulnerable to teachers' opinions when they have very low self-esteem.

There seems to be little point in becoming a teacher if you do not feel respect for the pupils you will be teaching, no matter what their levels of attainment. Respect for your pupils will be conveyed by the language you choose with which to address them, the phrases you use when questioning, instructing, managing and otherwise interacting with them, the volume and tone of voice you use at all times, and the impression you convey to them through your preparation, planning and running of your lessons that you have their best interests at heart.

The use of sarcasm, shouting and insults will not naturally lead pupils to think that you respect them, and may ultimately be counter-productive. Your respect for pupils needs to be rooted in your recognition of the responsibility you bear for their learning, and your recognition of the effect of lack of respect on them. There are many ways in which lack of respect manifests itself, but essentially where pupils pick up the message that they do not matter to the teacher, they will also recognize that they are not respected.

BEING CONSISTENT

Maintaining consistency is one of the most important ways in which pupils' behaviour can be managed and shaped. It is also essential for maintaining a secure learning environment within the classroom. Secondary pupils harbour a strong sense of justice, which adults can sometimes lose sight of, and a consistent response to the same instances and situations is one way in which teachers can ensure that pupils feel that they are being treated fairly. In managing the quite large numbers of individuals who make up most secondary classes, it is important that you have consistent and well-established routines and responses which provide the boundaries necessary for pupils' engagement and pro-learning behaviour.

Setting up rules, routines and codes of behaviour

Before you encounter new classes, it is necessary for you to have made decisions about the rules, routines and codes of behaviour you will expect to be adhered to in your classroom. Your rules should fall within the general policies operating in your school, as should your codes of behaviour. For example, schools require pupils to take off their coats in classrooms, to have pens, pencils and books ready and to put their bags out of the way. Chewing and eating are usually forbidden also. If you are working in a school where ready access to drinking water is encouraged, usually in the form of pupils' own bottles of water, then this should be an accepted part of your classroom routines.

Your routines will be personal to you, but typically will include how you manage the start and end of your lessons, how you manage the giving out of books and materials, how you ensure orderly movement round the classroom where this is necessary (for example when pupils need to move to the front to participate in a science demonstration), and how you routinely ensure the safety and health of pupils (for example, by taking account of the need for fresh air).

As with boundaries which are set to manage behaviour, routines are also very important to pupils in giving them a sense of security and purpose.

Setting up rules and codes of behaviour in consultation with pupils

This may not immediately appeal to you, and is not something to be done until you feel established and confident. This is not a common practice on the whole, but where it is used successfully, can produce a most cooperative and learning-centred atmosphere in the classroom.

The process of consultation is similar to the one used to establish criteria for learning and assessment in the assessment for learning practices; the problem, desired outcome and/or desired way of working are outlined to pupils, who are invited to suggest how this can best be brought about. With regard to setting up rules for a productive classroom environment, the teacher might ask pupils to come up with their answers to the following questions:

- How could we make sure that we have a good start to the lesson, with everyone here?
- What do we think we ought to have with us for each lesson to make sure that we get the most out of it?
- What ideas do we have about how instructions and lesson aims are given by the teacher?
- What ideas do we have about helping people who have not grasped the lesson?
- What kind of marking or assessment of our work would help us most during a lesson?
- Can we work out some rules for how to move about the room, how to get quiet, how to do group work?
- What rules should we have for the end of lessons?
- Which rules, the school's and the teacher's, must we stick to, whatever we feel about them? Why should we do this?

No doubt you could think of further questions. This might look like an impossibly idealistic way of working with pupils, but giving pupils the opportunity to become responsible for their own behaviour is more likely to produce autonomy than the imposition of external controls, some of which can appear to be quite arbitrary. However, this area can be quite contentious; it is offered for your consideration here, so you can be aware that there are alternative ways of managing the behaviour in your classroom.

HELPING PUPILS CALM DOWN

A way of calming younger pupils down at the start of a lesson following break or lunchtime, often very difficult for pupils and teachers, is to deliberately get the pupils to go to sleep. This somewhat startling request does not usually result in actual sleep, but does allow pupils to calm down. While their heads are on their tables, you can either very quietly talk them through something you wish them to think about, or what you want them to do when they sit up again, or even play them some music. The main reason for the success of this approach is that many pupils, especially younger ones, simply do not have the necessary skills to calm themselves down. Break and lunchtime, far from being pleasantly relaxed times for pupils, can often be the occasions for bullying, fighting and the rousing of high emotions, and because there is relatively little supervision, can leave pupils feeling vulnerable. They then bring all this into the next lesson, and naturally do not know how to cope with it. Used skilfully and with conviction, this method brings about a much greater sense of collaboration and cooperation within classes, and reassures pupils that their emotional needs are being recognized.

SUMMARY

In this chapter you are encouraged to:

- be informed about school behaviour policies;
- work with the support of others in dealing with inappropriate behaviour;
- work towards an understanding of what produces unacceptable behaviour;
- think carefully about your use of praise; find ways to avoid using empty words like 'good';
- consider your use of motivational strategies with all your classes;

- decide how you will convey your respect for pupils;
- consider the implications of being consistent, and whether you need to work on this;
- set up rules, routines and codes of behaviour, which you and your pupils agree on and abide by;
- develop some strategies to help pupils calm down.

STANDARDS

This chapter will help you consider some of the issues implicit in many of the standards in Section 3.3: Teaching and Class Management.

NOTES

1 This disorder is diagnosed in children exhibiting restlessness, inability to concentrate for more than a few minutes at a time, propensity to being easily distracted from something they are doing and can also lead to aggressive, irrational behaviour. One common form of treatment at the moment is the prescribing of medication. It is becoming increasingly common for even quite young children to be given such medication. It tends to be a disorder more commonly found in boys. Look at http://www.rcpsych.ac.uk/ and http://www.bbc.co.uk/health/conditons/attention2.shtml.

2 For a good resource on motivation see McLean, A. (2003), The Motivated School. London: Paul Chapman Publishing, which discusses motivation from a wide range of perspectives and in a detailed, informative and helpful way.

Chapter 9

Course books, text books, worksheets and ICT

This chapter offers some suggestions with regard to your use of materials and resources in your teaching, focusing on the reading challenges which such resources may pose for pupils.

COURSE BOOKS AND TEXT BOOKS

For many subjects, use of some course books is necessary and built into schemes of work. However, course and text books cannot on their own guarantee successful lessons, though they can undoubtedly contribute to them.

For your own subject, it is worth spending some time investigating the following aspects of such materials before embarking on using them in your lessons:

- the layout;
- visuals as a proportion of the total page;
- printed text as a proportion of the total page;
- the language used in the printed text;
- the intellectual and cognitive demands you consider the text makes of its readers;
- your preparedness to make use of the materials in your teaching;

- your evaluation of the usefulness of the materials in promoting your pupils' learning and understanding.

The layout

Course book publishers and editors appear to have decided that the more 'attractive' the layout and presentation of a page, the better for pupils – or maybe, the more likely that teachers will buy a set of the books. Try to look objectively at a sample page and evaluate what it expects of its readers, from the point of view of how the page is laid out, and from the point of view of pupils who may not be totally confident readers. For example, the page may operate in a recursive rather than a linear way, so the reader is encouraged to engage in very small chunks of reading, possibly in insets or boxes, and also in looking at visuals and their subtitles, in no particular order. The conventional presentation of printed text in English, requiring the reader to move from top to bottom and left to right, is entirely disrupted in texts of this kind. How is the less confident reader expected to tackle this? However, the text may be presented in a linear way, requiring a conventional reading process, but possibly interrupted or accompanied by visuals.

Visuals as a proportion of the total page

Visuals are obviously an important part of all teaching, so it is important that you understand how they work, and how you can ensure that your pupils can 'read' them. It is tempting to take for granted pupils' ability to understand and interpret visual information because of their assumed familiarity with media representations, and their undoubted sophistication in responding to certain kinds of media artefact. However, the particular conventions operating in course and text books are not the same, and it is necessary for you to interrogate such materials from the point of view of the pupil. Are they visuals which only convey meaning if pupils have prior knowledge of how they work, such as graphs, maps, plans, diagrams, charts, tables and lists? Are they visuals which appear easy to interpret, such as photographs, paintings, line drawings and cartoons, but which actually make a range of 'reading' demands on inexperienced pupils which they will need help with? All these considerations are particularly important in classes with pupils from cultural backgrounds other than white British, in which particular constraints and beliefs about visual representations may well operate.

It is also necessary for you to decide what use you wish to make of the visuals on any page you are working on with pupils. You will need to decide how much time, if any, you want your pupils to spend on looking at and discussing visuals, and what use you will want to make of the information or perspective offered by them. You may need to be quite ruthless about this, but on the other hand you may decide that the visuals offer the best chance for all pupils to take something in terms of learning from the lesson.

Printed text as a proportion of the total page

The proportion of printed text on each page will be related, as with visuals, to the general purpose of each page and its contribution to the overall intended learning of the course book. Less text may seem an attractive proposition to many teachers and pupils, but it is worth your considering whether in the long run this helps pupils. More focus on interpreting and responding to lengthier and more substantial printed text might well help pupils develop a range of reading skills, including the ability to interpret and challenge, which may not be developed elsewhere in the school curriculum. You should be wary, in all instances of working with such texts, of taking for granted that pupils have understood them. In a small piece of unpublished research conducted with some Year 7 pupils, in which a wide range of course books from different subjects was looked at and discussed, it was clear that in spite of their protestations that they understood the pages they were looking at, in fact they did not. Nor did they have any learned strategies for checking their understanding, or recognizing where they had misunderstood specific words or vocabulary.

The challenge for you as a teacher is to decide how you will use the printed text component of pages you are working on, and how much preparation you will need to do to ensure that all your pupils understand what they are being asked to read and respond to. Often it can be more productive to use course books as secondary materials, to be read and responded to after you have already engaged pupils in the content in a different way. It is very difficult for pupils to immediately engage in the content of a piece of text without planned support from teachers.

The language used in the printed text

Most texts of the kind being discussed here present some pupils with significant problems of understanding, usually because of the language used. It will repay you to spend time seeing for yourself just what these challenges might be in a piece of text you intend to use. As a general rule, these language problems can be categorized thus:

- The syntax is difficult or unfamiliar to pupils; that is, sentences have multiple subclauses, and thus are complex rather than compound or simple, and require reading approaches that less confident readers will not yet have mastered.
- The writers have made assumptions (necessarily) about their readers' prior knowledge and understanding.
- The vocabulary is unfamiliar to pupils: this can be because specialist, subject-specific vocabulary is unfamiliar to pupils, or because the general lexis of the text is beyond their experience.
- The language used to accompany the visuals may also be unfamiliar to pupils.

It is easy as a teacher to make assumptions about what pupils know and understand in terms of sentence structure and syntax, specialist and general vocabulary, and it takes time to learn how to recognize the likely features of any text you are using which will present pupils with problems. It is worth planning with a class of pupils an investigation into some pages of a course book you are using, so that the pupils themselves can highlight for you what they find difficult. Given the reluctance of pupils to acknowledge that they have problems in understanding, this exercise might be worth carrying out by putting the pupils in the role of evaluators making recommendations to the publisher about how to revise the text for future pupils. In this way they can be encouraged to focus on what they have found difficult, and will also be able to take a more objective view of it. This approach also encourages pupils to feel much more engaged in their own learning. From the results of this exercise, which could be done in one lesson and might well have very important results for you in terms of pupils' motivation, you will be able to reach useful conclusions pointing to the kind of preparation or alternative practice you will need to do in future.

Literacy across the Curriculum initiatives have had some effect on the ways in which teachers of subjects other than English now understand the kinds of language they are expecting their pupils to use and understand. Many teachers have word walls in their classrooms, on which are displayed key words for the subject. This means that pupils can often spell such words correctly, where they are still making errors with 'ordinary' vocabulary. This does not mean, however, that pupils necessarily understand what these words mean, nor that they make use of word walls unless this is made a very explicit part of classroom practice.

The intellectual and cognitive demands you consider the text makes of its readers

The intellectual and cognitive content of a course or text book is probably the first aspect of it by which you will judge its suitability. You are likely to decide whether your pupils will, or will not, understand these aspects of the text, and will look for something more suitable where necessary. It is worth deciding just what helped you reach your conclusions about the book. It is possible that the intellectual and cognitive content was not particularly difficult in itself, but was presented in an unhelpful way. In this case it probably could be used so that pupils could understand it, by using different methods of presentation and explanation. It is also possible that the intellectual and cognitive content was too advanced for pupils at that particular stage of their education, and that they would need more support before tackling that content.

Whatever conclusions you reach about this, it is important that you ensure that the text does the job you expect of it: that is, that it develops and encourages pupils' thinking and learning, and does not present insuperable barriers to them.

Your preparedness to make use of the materials in your teaching

Having done all this preparatory work on the text you wish to use, you still need to work out how you will embed it in your lesson plan. You will need to decide what kind of reading of the text is going to occur, and how you are going to organize your pupils to do it. You obviously have several options:

- Read the text yourself.
- Read the text round the class, asking for answers to questions, and encouraging some discussion of the text.
- Grouping or pairing pupils to examine small parts of the text and report back to the whole class.
- Asking pupils to read the text silently on their own, and then be prepared to ask and answer questions on it.

In all these cases, you need to think through the pedagogical implications of what you are intending to do: which of these methods, or others you may choose, are most likely to engage all the pupils, and enable them to reach the learning outcomes of the lesson? You will also need to be quite certain about how much of the text you intend to use, and why; what will this contribute to pupils' learning that other methods could not achieve?

You will also need to have fully prepared the text, so that you are in a position to deal with any problems, and are aware of aspects which will need extra attention from you to help pupils gain from the text what you intended.

Your evaluation of the usefulness of the materials in promoting your pupils' learning and understanding

In most subject departments in secondary schools, a certain amount of leeway is given to teachers to decide how they want to prepare their teaching materials and approaches. You may never need to use a course or text book, or you may choose never to do so. For many subjects this is probably rather unlikely; at the very least you will probably use specific extracts from such materials in order to support pupils' learning of specific content. Whatever is the case, you are likely to make quite quick judgements of these materials in terms of their usefulness in promoting learning and understanding. It is worth spending a little time making more detailed evaluations of this sort, as they will not only help you evaluate the materials, but also help you develop your understanding of pedagogical practices which you deploy when you are not using such materials.

One of the typical problems you will find with course books is that they reflect their writers' experiences of pupils and classroom teaching, but these are not necessarily appropriate for your own pupils and teaching. Whether you choose to use them or not, you do need to recognize that you cannot simply walk into a classroom with a pile of course books, set the pupils to work in some fashion or other, and expect this to produce learning. Above all, you must avoid the 'lazy teacher syndrome' of asking pupils to 'turn to page xx in your book and copy out paragraphs xx and then do a drawing'.

WORKSHEETS

The alternative to course books for many lessons is worksheets. Worksheets can raise all sorts of 'political' and departmental problems, as well as the obvious ones produced for pupils in lessons. 'Political' problems can be raised where a member or members of a department routinely produce high quality worksheets which other non-productive members of the department expect to be able to use, without in any way reciprocating. Such problems can also arise if the worksheets in question are demonstrably better then anything produced by the head of department. Departmental problems can arise with regard to shared access, storage, photocopying costs and general departmental policy on materials. You may come across departments where worksheets are strongly discouraged, and others where pupils are in danger of 'death by worksheet'. Where cost is an issue, it is worth preparing worksheets which can be reused many times. If your lesson involves pupils making direct responses to worksheet questions or problems, devise ways in which these responses do not have to be written directly onto the worksheet.

The best practice with regard to worksheets is for all members of a department to be involved in a regular way in producing them collaboratively, and for the worksheets to be stored centrally for easy access by everyone.

Good worksheets fulfil a range of functions and purposes. They:

- make clear their learning intentions;
- provide a carefully thought through focus on the content to be learned;
- are deliberately shaped to allow pupils to develop their understanding as they go along;
- challenge pupils to think and question;
- encourage pupils to think of alternatives;
- encourage pupils to make contributions to plenary or other discussions.

Time-filling worksheets, in other words the antithesis of good worksheets:

- give pupils a lot to do but little to think about;
- encourage activities such as drawing which have no discernible link with any learning;
- pose few or no challenges;
- are intended to keep pupils quiet and 'occupied', and not planned to bring about any learning;
- are rarely if ever used for evaluation of learning.

When you prepare your own worksheets, and preferably you will word-process them, you do need to keep at the front of your mind the following:

- What is the learning purpose of this worksheet?
- How should I lay it out and organize it to ensure that this learning purpose can be met?
- What is the best layout to use?
- Have I ensured that it contains no spelling errors?
- Have I ensured that it is presented professionally?

In addition to worksheets, it is worth mentioning here the importance of careful preparation and presentation of materials, such as photocopies. At all times you should demonstrate your respect for your pupils and their learning by ensuring that what you present them with has been produced to the highest standard you can obtain. There is nothing worse than photocopied materials that are illegible, either because the photocopier was misbehaving that day, or because you could not be bothered to cut and paste, or because you photocopied something in a very small font size and did not bother to increase it as you copied. It is also not good practice to present pupils with material which has clearly been downloaded from a website and simply been copied as it stood.

USE OF ICT AS A TEACHING AID

This section is focused on your use of ICT as a teaching aid, rather than on your pupils as users of ICT during your lessons. Access to ICT in schools cannot be taken for granted, and for many teachers and their classes the opportunities to work in computer rooms for any appreciable length of time are few. You are more likely to be able to use ICT as a focus for teaching and learning by using an interactive whiteboard in your classroom. This section offers some very general suggestions about such use.

There is no doubt that pupils respond well to any kind of screen visuals; TV, video recordings and whiteboards all grab their attention and usually hold it for substantial periods of time. The key consideration for you is whether they are actively learning anything from these experiences or are merely kept occupied by them. Interactive whiteboards do differ, of course, in the teaching approaches they make possible, and as with all resources, your planning for their optimum use is of key importance. It is becoming increasingly common for teachers to use PowerPoint presentations instead of printed texts in the exposition of content, and many also use this opportunity to encourage the close engagement of their pupils. As with printed texts, such presentations make reading demands, though of a different nature, on pupils, and these need to be carefully considered before pupils are exposed to them. The sequences of the exposition also need to be very carefully thought through before their use in lessons, to ensure that pupils will follow the underlying thread of what you are aiming at.

In preparing for any use of ICT in the classroom, you should weigh the expected educational benefit against the preparation time involved before you decide to go ahead. Using ICT for the sake of using ICT is pointless; there is some point when you know that it will foster learning that otherwise would be much more difficult to bring about. As you prepare, bear in mind the following:

- your time input compared with your pupils' learning outcomes;
- the actual learning outcomes made possible by using ICT, including the intellectual demands this will make on pupils;
- what you expect your pupils to do in response to each phase of your presentation;
- how you will conduct the necessary talk in relation to the presentation;
- your expertise in manipulating the technology;
- whether you are using ICT to impress others rather than teach your pupils;
- the classroom organization necessary for optimum learning.

Every time you consider using ICT in any way at all with your pupils, ask yourself this very simple question: 'does what I want my pupils to do go through the brain?'

SUMMARY

In this chapter, you are encouraged to:

- consider key features of printed texts such as course books and text books in relation to your pupils' ability to understand them;
- work out in an informed way how you will use printed texts with your pupils;
- decide whether you need to use such texts at all;
- prepare worksheets and resources carefully and professionally;
- carefully consider your use of ICT for promoting learning.

STANDARDS

This chapter will help you consider some of the issues implicit in the following standards. Trainees:

2.5;   know how to use ICT effectively;

3.1.3;   select and prepare resources;

3.3.8;   organize and manage materials, texts and other resources effectively;

3.3.10; use ICT effectively in teaching.

Chapter 10

Schemes of work and lesson planning

This chapter considers some of the implications of planning schemes of work and individual lessons, recognizing that these form the organizational basis of your classroom work and preparation.

SCHEMES OF WORK

In many departments, the advent of the National Curriculum, and the pressures placed on schools by the demands of the Ofsted inspection processes, have resulted in schemes of work which in more or less detail outline what is to be taught to each year group term by term (or often half-term by half-term) through the year. These schemes are designed to help teachers put into practice the demands of the National Curriculum, and of examination specifications, and a great deal of work has usually gone into them. You may yourself have been engaged in helping to produce such schemes during your training year.

The point of schemes of work is to enable you to see at a glance what you will need to be planning and preparing for week by week over a set period, usually a half-term, and they thus allow you to think ahead; this is particularly useful if any out-of-school work or visits are part of the scheme.

To enable you to produce your own schemes of work, the following advice is offered:

- think backwards: start at the end, by ensuring that you know and understand the intended final learning outcomes for the period of the scheme. These are highly likely to be some of the National Curriculum requirements for your subject;
- subdivide the desired learning outcomes for the whole scheme into smaller units, achievable in a shorter space of time – a week, or a group of lessons;
- consider each learning outcome individually and make a list of all its component parts: cognitive learning, skills (as listed below in the subsection on lesson planning), practical outcomes and evidence, how you will assess that each learning outcome has been achieved;
- plan an outline of how each of these component parts can be linked together, with continuity and progression across lessons. In some instances this will be self-evident because of the particular nature of the learning outcomes; in others, particularly in subject areas with a more fluid organization, this will need more detailed consideration;
- map your outline onto the organizational plan used in your department; this may be a lesson-by-lesson grid, or a week-by-week outline, or even a more general half-term outline.

You will still need to plan and prepare each individual lesson, but the scheme of work should make this process much easier. Throughout your planning, no matter for what purpose, your initial questions should be:

- What am I expecting/wanting/needing my pupils to learn/gain from this work?
- How can I ensure that this happens?
- How am I going to know at the end that it has happened?

This approach encourages you to think in a purposeful way about the end point of your teaching, particularly the learning aims of your lessons, and encourages a different kind of pedagogically based thinking.

It is worth remembering that Ofsted inspectors base some of their judgements about how well a department and individual teachers are performing on the efficiency and validity of their planning procedures and documentation.

LESSON PLANNING

How to analyse the stages inherent in learning processes

Unpicking what you know and how you know it is central to the ways in which you operate as a teacher. If you can think yourself into the position of the learner, as opposed to the position of the knower, you are well on the way to effective planning. This is quite a challenging process; it can be difficult to imagine yourself into the minds of your pupils, and all too easy to assume that they see things in the same way that you do. It is useful to remember that all your pupils will be approaching your lessons from a rather different viewpoint from your own, and from a completely different range of reference and experience. It is therefore important that you learn how to identify useful starting points for the learning you are planning for, and in many instances these can be given to you by pupils themselves.

A useful technique to help you, and one which is also used with pupils, is to ask a series of questions, on these lines:

- What do we already know about . . . ?
- What more do we need to know?
- How can we find out?
- What skills will we need to do this?
- How can we learn these skills?
- How will we know we have acquired the skills and learned the content?

The answers to these questions can provide a useful planning framework, and at the same time give opportunities to think learning through in stages, including the evaluation necessary at the end of the process. This process also involves pupils in thinking about their learning, as opposed to being passive receivers of what the teacher decides to tell them.

Developing learning from previous lessons

Pupils will have been expected to engage in a lot of other, possibly quite different learning since your last lesson with them. It is therefore wise to make no assumptions about what they have remembered; however brilliant your last lesson was, and however much pupils enjoyed it and learned from it, they will not bring to your next lesson the same expectations that you might have.

You therefore need to develop ways of quickly engaging pupils in appraisals and recapitulations of what they did accomplish in the previous lesson. This should then form a useful basis for showing pupils what the current lesson will aim to teach them, and will give you opportunities to help pupils see how their learning within your subject area is being promoted in a developmental, progressive way. The more you help pupils construct a meaningful context for their learning, the more likely you are to be successful in teaching them

At this point it is useful to point out that question-and-answer sessions which only involve a few pupils in the class are not a good way of establishing what has already been learned, or anything else for that matter. It is not a good idea to think that because a few pupils have come up with the kind of answer you were looking for, that the rest of the class have been listening, have understood, have been able to link what others have said with their own memories of the last lesson (if they have any) or that you are doing anything other than making yourself feel that you've done something positive. Questioning, as indicated elsewhere, needs to be much more carefully thought out and used.

Whether or not your last lesson was a success, it is always a good idea to rethink your approach to the next lesson; trying to repeat successful approaches does not always work, and it is sensible to consider other ways of engaging pupils in the next lesson, so that they do not come to expect the same thing every time they enter your classroom. Varied approaches keep pupils interested and guessing, and can be deliberately discussed with pupils as part of a general approach designed to engage them fully in their own learning.

At some stage of your work with pupils it is very useful to give them the opportunity to tell you how they learn most effectively, and to use this information to help you in your future planning. It can also be really interesting for pupils to learn about how the brain takes in and makes use of new learning, and how the gap between one lesson and the next can be really useful to allow new learning to be assimilated. The more pupils know about how learning takes place the better.

What pupils already know

It is advisable to include in your planning the time (and the relevant strategies) to elicit from pupils what they already know about the content and skills to be addressed in any one lesson. In this respect, planning needs to be done as carefully as for the main body of your lesson. There is little point in asking pupils *directly* what they know, or have already done. In many cases, even though you may have been informed by their previous teacher that they have 'done' something in previous lessons, pupils are highly likely to deny that they have ever heard of it, and many will profess to having no idea what you are talking about. You will find the same thing happening with regard to lessons which you have taught them yourself.

This means that you need to devise ways of starting your lessons which actively engage pupils in remembering what they have already done, and in which there is some incentive for them to convince you of how well they already know it, or can do it. Such activities can often be embedded in starters, and can be most effective when they allow pupils to reengage in the concerns of your subject area. It has to be remembered that pupils in school do not generally spend their time thinking about your subject to the exclusion of all else; they are forced to switch focus and to think differently at least four times each day, depending on their timetables, and between each of your lessons with a class they could have attended lessons in at least six different subjects. This makes starting activities all the more important, and also serves to show pupils that you have their interests at heart, and that you recognize that they need this kind of help to focus on your lesson.

You do also have to be prepared for pupils to attempt to derail your lesson by either claiming to have done this all before, or denying that they did it in your last lesson and that they therefore know anything at all about subtraction, metals, water erosion, the French for 'I go to the shops and buy a banana', subclauses or how to spell key words. So you have to be prepared to find a balance between *assuming absolutely nothing* about what pupils already know, and being ready to acknowledge the startling things they do know.

Some of the most effective methods for this part of the lesson are:

- pupils showing what they already know on the board;
- simple competitions to see who can remember key points;
- pupils in pairs writing down 'at least five' things from the last lesson in two minutes;
- pupils being given a worksheet to complete with key items from the last lesson.

A more sophisticated approach is to make remembering and recalling learning from previous lessons an integral and expected part of each new lesson. One way to do this is to designate pupils, possibly in pairs, to be responsible for giving their peers a quick synopsis of the previous lesson, from the front of the class. This technique increases pupils' sense of the importance of what they are doing, develops their recall, helps them see your lessons as part of a developmental whole, and gives them responsibility not just for their own learning but for that of their peers. However you cater for this aspect of your lessons, it is important that you acknowledge its key place in your planning.

Pupils' concentration spans

It is useful to remember that most people, including children, have an upper time span for listening with concentration and understanding, beyond which they cease to take anything in. Much teaching methodology takes account of this, and advises that pupils are given small 'chunks' of activity and learning, and that teachers avoid talking at them for long periods. While this is undoubtedly an effective method with many pupils in the sense of keeping them engaged and on task, it does little to develop their concentration spans and nothing at all to help them understand the level of commitment needed for higher levels of study.

Your lesson planning, therefore, needs to take account of pupils' levels of concentration in a variety of contexts, and at different times of the day and week. An exciting and interesting lesson will probably elicit greater concentration than a more prosaic, 'boring' lesson, though they may be equally valid educationally. Your planning should also explicitly address concentration levels by making overt demands on pupils in terms of intensity of activity, the time allocated to activities and rigorous outcomes.

Meaningful contexts for pupils

As human beings operate in the world by using all the cues available to them to make sense of their surroundings, it seems sensible to give pupils in school as many cues as possible, in order that they can make better use of their lessons. This may require quite a shift in your thinking: there is a very strong tradition in teaching in England of not making pupils fully aware of what they are engaged in, even though writing lesson objectives on the board has become very common practice and is intended to overcome the problem. In spite of this, much of what teachers present to pupils can appear to be quite arbitrary; a teacher's decision to 'do' a particular bit of the curriculum in a lesson obviously makes sense to the teacher, but does not always make sense to pupils.

The more you help your pupils understand the overall context in which they are expected to learn, the more likely you are to help them be successful. These contexts can be thought of in several ways:

- short term: the context for one lesson, in relation to the previous lesson and the next lesson;
- medium term: the context for a half-term's worth of lessons, which you can give to pupils in the form of a simple timetable;

- longer term: the context for the year. Again, you can give pupils a timetable for this, so that they know where you are taking them in their learning between September and July;
- assessment context: you ensure that pupils know the kinds and dates of formal assessments at the start of the year, and include in your timetable opportunities for preparation for these assessments.

The advantage to you of planning like this is that you always know in advance what lessons you will be preparing for, and your pupils will be able to develop a much greater degree of autonomy with regard to their understanding of where they are going and why. You probably already have access to such medium- and longer-term plans; the idea is to make them accessible to your pupils.

Knowing your learning objectives

For all your lesson planning, you need to be very clear about:

- the learning objectives for each lesson;
- where each lesson fits into the learning objectives of the scheme of work;
- how your learning objectives are intended to move pupils on;
- how you will shape the lesson to enable the learning objectives to be reached;
- how you will use materials, resources and other aids to support the attainment of your learning objectives;
- how you will use assessment of different kinds during and after the lesson to ensure that all pupils are given the necessary opportunities to reach the learning objectives.

This approach to lesson planning is a useful way to ensure that your focus is on learning. It is perfectly possible, and indeed not uncommon, for lessons to be conducted on the principle of pupils 'doing' things, with or without the implicit belief on the part of the teacher that anything will actually be learned. As with planning for schemes of work, it is a good idea to start your lesson planning from the end of the lesson, and work backwards from what you expect pupils to have learned, constantly asking yourself the question: 'What steps will I need to take my pupils through so that they will reach this learning objective?'

Matching lesson planning to wider objectives

As well as identifying the learning objectives for individual lessons, you need to keep an eye on the larger overall objectives which underpin the scheme of work or examination specification within which you are working. One-off lesson planning is not conducive to this developmental model, and it is therefore better to think through and plan your lessons in appropriate groupings with a clear focus on the overall outcomes you are aiming at.

Lesson planning related to external tests and examinations

Tests and examinations results are the predominant means whereby schools are judged, and judge themselves. Results of tests and examinations determine schools' positions in league tables, and play a large part in Ofsted designation of schools. For 11–18 schools, pupils' performance at GCSE has come to be the end point and purpose of everything that the school as an institution undertakes. The investment in tests and examinations is enormous, both financially and in terms of time and effort.

Therefore, in planning schemes of work and lessons for pupils being entered for tests and examinations, you obviously need to know the subject content to be taught, which you will find in the relevant specifications given by each of the three main examination boards: AQA, OCR and Edexcel. The tests for Key Stage 3 in English, mathematics and science prescribe content and testing methods with some choice for the teacher or department of the content to be taught. GCSE examinations at the end of Key Stage 4 also offer choices within the prescribed content. Decisions about which content is to be taught at both levels are usually made by departments as a whole, and can be governed by a range of factors, including availability of teaching materials, the wishes of individual teachers, the needs of pupils and the pressure to achieve the highest percentage of GCSE passes possible.

It is a good idea to read your subject specifications carefully, and in particular to familiarize yourself with the assessment objectives of the examination. (It is useful to look at the examination specifications alongside the National Curriculum for Key Stage 4 for your subject in order to see how closely linked the content and assessment requirements are.) Planning for teaching pupils for examinations is best done by taking careful note of the assessment objectives in conjunction with the prescribed content. This will all obviously be important in your overall lesson planning and preparation. It is worth thinking about the relationship between the assessment objectives and the content of examination specifications in your subject area. Essentially, assessment objectives provide a useful set of learning outcomes, and can be used as the first point of consideration when you are planning your schemes of work. Assessment objectives offer a succinct overview of the knowledge and skills which the examination is designed to test. Obvious though it might be, it is worth pointing out that if your teaching has not enabled your pupils to meet the assessment objectives, they are unlikely to fare very well in the examinations.

It is very helpful for your pupils if you also have some idea of what they are being expected to do in other areas of the curriculum with regard to tests and examinations as well as your own. Largely because of the pressure on schools to increase their pass rate at GCSE, teaching to the test or examination has become a high stakes priority. You might like to think about the effect on pupils of 'teaching to the test', and to consider what kind of teaching and education this is.

Pedagogical understanding and behaviour management techniques within your planning

As you become more experienced you will obviously not need to include in your lesson plans the exact detail of what you intend for every minute of the lesson. However, on your road to becoming skilled and professional, it is useful to spend time thinking through this kind of detail, and considering how conducive to your pupils' learning your intended approaches are likely to be. Chapter 7 (Managing learning) and Chapter 8 (Managing behaviour) will be useful in conjunction with this chapter, to help you think through the approaches most likely to produce the learning outcomes you are aiming for with each particular class.

It is good pedagogical practice to engage pupils in evaluating the lesson, as part of a plenary session in which they are invited to think back over the lesson and comment on its usefulness to them. For example, you might ask them to talk about:

- what they thought the lesson plan included, and its aims;
- points at which they would have liked more opportunities to ask questions or discuss;
- points at which they felt lost and needed more explanation;
- parts of the lesson plan which they think did not work;
- parts of the lesson which they enjoyed;
- what they think they *really* learned from the lesson (as opposed to saying 'yes' to all the learning objectives you have so carefully written on the board before the start of the lesson).

Catering for all your pupils

As you become familiar with your classes, you will of course identify the differences between your pupils in terms of their readiness for lessons, their willingness to participate, the previous learning they are able to bring to bear in each lesson, their skill levels in reading and writing, other skills they can deploy, their articulacy and general outward attitude. Your acuity in picking up and storing all this information is likely to be well developed, and it is therefore important that you use it creatively, purposefully and positively. It is very easy to *judge* pupils, and to move on from that to categorize and label them. You do need to be wary of not allowing yourself to fall into the trap of modifying and lowering your expectations of your pupils in relation to your own categorization. In order for your teaching to be successful, your expectations need to remain high, even unrealistically high; your pupils need to be helped to rise beyond their current levels, both in performance and self-expectation. The challenge is not only to find ways of doing this, but to *believe* in the necessity of doing it.

DEPARTING FROM YOUR LESSON PLAN

Experienced teachers know how to exploit learning and teaching opportunities which arise in an unplanned way in the course of lessons. They are able to incorporate them into the lesson, and still manage to adhere to the general aim of the lesson. A useful label for these 'teaching events' is 'incidental teaching'. Until you have reached this stage of professionalism, it is important that you don't put yourself in such potentially difficult situations. In many subject areas, this departure from the lesson plan is less likely to occur than in others, because of the nature of the activities, and the need for tight planning, as in subjects requiring the use of apparatus.

Departing from lesson plans can also be caused by more negative and potentially confidence-sapping situations, which may include the following:

- you lose the thread of what you were trying to do, because you were not experienced enough to 'learn' your lesson plan and keep it in your head;
- planned activities take far longer than you had allowed for and you don't know how to handle the effect this will have on your overall lesson;
- the lesson does not run smoothly from the start, due to a variety of factors such as late arrival of pupils, constant interruptions, unacceptable behaviour from some pupils, homework not done, late start to the lesson because of other school-based factors;
- you realize too late that pupils have already covered the content of your plan.

In these circumstances, some of them unforeseen and therefore not allowed for in your planning, it is advisable to curtail your aims for that lesson, but still keep to your usual lesson pattern, so that for example, you have a plenary, and you manage the ending of your lesson in such a way that pupils can see you are still in control. It may be possible to turn the missed lesson content into homework, but it is generally not a good idea to allow pupils to feel that they are being 'punished' in this way for events for which they were not responsible.

Mostly, you should know in advance about planned disruptions to lessons, such as long assemblies, pupils being taken out of lessons by other staff for various reasons, or some pupils but not the whole class out on a trip and so on, and should make due allowance for them in your planning.

In many situations where lessons have not gone according to plan, a certain amount of improvisation needs to be put into effect; this means that in your planning you will need to have thought through just what you will do in the kind of situation outlined above. It is a good idea to acquire as you go through your training and career a repertoire of 'useful things to do in an emergency'. These may include little tests, competitions, spellings, games related to the learning objectives and word games. In addition, it is vital that you consciously acquire the kind of strategies that experienced teachers seem able to deploy at will, and that you learn how and when to use them. An example from a trainee's English lesson illustrates this well. The trainee had come to the end of an engaging lesson based on pupils' responses to a simple ballad. Pupils had been thoroughly engrossed in the lesson, and the trainee was feeling very pleased, both with the pupils and with himself. Then he realized with horror that he had totally misjudged the time, and thought he had come to the end of the lesson when he in fact had another ten minutes to go. He floundered at this stage, not having yet acquired any of the strategies mentioned above. His mentor quickly whispered to him from the back of the room to ask pupils whether they could say any of the lines of the ballad, which they had heard several times during the lesson. Immediately, the pupils responded enthusiastically to this challenge, and actually showed that they had remembered a great deal.

This anecdote illustrates how the simplest strategies can have the most positive outcome. Without using this idea, the trainee's lesson would have ground to a halt in a most ignominious way and the pupils would have become increasingly restless.

HOW TO BUILD AN OPTIMUM SEQUENCE FOR INDIVIDUAL LESSONS

For many lessons, the order in which each part of the lesson will need to occur is fairly obvious because of the nature of the scheme of work being covered. It is usual for lessons to be planned on the basis of an assumption that learning will occur in a linear fashion. This assumption may also extend to schemes of work as a whole, and indeed to the whole curriculum. It is worth reminding yourself, however, that the National Curriculum tends to avoid prescribing an *order* in which content should be taught and so teachers do have to decide this for themselves.

Individual lessons often follow a general pattern which exemplifies a kind of unspoken consensus about what teaching and learning should be about. This pattern can be presented in very general terms in this way:

- the start of the lesson includes some kind of recapitulation of pupils' previous learning or of previous lessons from which pupils may or may not have learned anything; it may also include discussion of pupils' ideas about the new content to be introduced;
- the objectives of the lesson are introduced by the teacher, maybe before the above, and the teacher checks for general understanding of these by asking a few pupils what they think the objectives mean. The teacher may link these objectives to the discussion which has just occurred;
- the teacher introduces the new content, in a variety of ways depending on the subject area, in the course of which pupils' understanding is checked in a variety of ways, which may or may not include some kind of response;
- if the content requires pupils to engage in some kind of task, which may include group or pair work, this then follows, and may also involve the teacher in moving around the room to offer help and advice. The teacher may give time limits for this work;
- at the time limit, the teacher brings the class together; this may be followed by some kind of sharing: discussion, showing completed work, demonstrating and explaining, which may then be followed

by some attempt to sum up, draw conclusions, extrapolate key points for future application, as in a plenary session;

- the teacher signals the end of the lesson, and follows pre-set routines for dismissing the class.

The basic pattern here is: check previous learning, introduce new learning, give opportunities for new learning to be practised or investigated, discuss findings or share experiences, draw some conclusions which can be applied in the future. This is clearly a linear model, and in many lessons and for many pupils it may well bring some measure of success. It is also the easiest model to plan for, in terms of sequence, though you do need to be very clear about the links between your learning objectives, the content and the activities you will be asking pupils to engage in.

A simple example of the thinking and planning inherent in this process based on a set of English lessons for Year 9 pupils, from which the key planning and thinking points for the first lesson are given, is as follows.

Media in English

Desired learning overall: pupils learn that storyboarding is a key method employed in the construction of a wide range of media artefacts, including film, TV drama, advertisements and cartoons, and understand why this is so. They can talk critically about the importance of story-boarding in relation to the intended screen picture to be presented to viewers.

Desired learning outcome for the lesson: pupils to understand how to: segment an extract from a short story; storyboard four of the segments; explain their choices and decisions in the light of the intended purpose and audience.

Thinking about this: by the end of this lesson I want my pupils to show me that they understand and can do the above. How should the lesson be shaped to help them reach this point?

I need to identify the skills they will need to deploy, which are:

1. knowing how to read the short story for the desired purpose;
2. knowing how to segment the given section;
3. knowing how to decide on perspectives and angles suggested by the segments;
4. being able to turn these into recognizable and useable storyboards which take account of the desired purpose and audience.

How to do this? The easiest way to do this would be to use a simple story, from which the pupils can learn the basics of this whole process, and then develop this in a more sophisticated way in a later lesson. So, I'll use a fairy tale, maybe *Cinderella*, and focus on how to segment just one section of the story. I shall also need to give them the intended audience and purpose: in this case the purpose will be the first storyboards for a cartoon version of *Cinderella* designed for quite young children.

I'll set up the reading so that pupils know what to focus on right from the start, and why we are doing it this way. Once I've introduced this to them, we'll read a version of the story up to the point where Cinderella is alone, wishing that she too could go to the Prince's ball. I'll ensure that they know what to be looking out for as we read, but we'll need to read this more than once, so each reading should enable them to focus more narrowly on suitable segments. Maybe this would take too long; I'll need to keep a tight rein on this part of the lesson.

I'll do this by:

- introducing the story very quickly, reminding them of it, and introducing it to pupils who may not know it;
- explaining what we are using the story for;
- explaining how I am going to read the story to help them decide how to segment it;
- explaining that when we have decided how to segment it, we will consider separately the features of storyboards.

I could give them choices about segments, but I am not going to because in this lesson what is important is that they learn some principles of segmenting, not that they have choices. I will also say that we are going to plan four segments only.

I will read the story several times: before the first reading, I'll ask them to listen out for the main events; after the first reading I'll ask them to tell me what they thought they were. I'll write these on the board, but before I do I'll ask them to suggest the most useful way of doing this. I'll steer them towards the idea of a table. Then I'll read the story again, asking them to listen out for some details of the main events. After this reading, I'll ask pupils to give me details, and maybe invite individuals up to the board to write their details in the table. Then I'll read the story again, quite slowly, and ask them to judge whether they think we have got the main events and details right, or would they like to change them or add to them. Again, pupils can come up to the board to add in their ideas.

At this stage we'll have a mini-plenary, to discuss how we have come up with our segments: what did we do? could we use the same techniques with other, longer texts? what difficulties might there be? It will be useful for them to note down in their books the techniques we have arrived at for segmenting, which they can apply in later lessons.

Now we'll explore the idea of storyboards, but I'll need to ensure that they continue to use the table on the board as our raw material. I will explain what a storyboard is and give them one example to consider, and then we'll model between us, on the board, a very simple single storyboard, which pupils will also contribute to, either by making suggestions or by coming up to the board to add their ideas, based on the first segment we have chosen. This will allow us to see that a storyboard has to include what people say, and other sound effects.

I'll need to introduce the idea of camera angles also at this stage. The example we have already used will help here, so we could produce a storyboard based on their suggestions about how to present the opening of the story. (I must remember to find a good example for this.) We'll need to talk about the difference that presentation makes to one image, which we can mock up on the board, and talk about how it would be read by the viewer, e.g. with the opening storyboard of Cinderella sitting in the primitive kitchen, maybe with a mountain of work to do. How do we want our viewers to respond? Do we want them to feel sorry for Cinderella? Yes. So how would we need to present her? What angle and type of shot would produce this effect? We'll need to discuss this, and I can also introduce the idea of the conventions used in visual presentations – Cinderella made to look small, vulnerable and pitiable by using an overhead angle, or by emphasizing the size of her task, again making her look small by using a middle distance shot where she is at the back of the picture overcome by the task mountain.

At this stage we need to have another mini-plenary to review where we have got to and what we have learned. I'm now thinking that we will not have time for each pupil to complete storyboards for each segment, so the task will be set up from the beginning for each group of four pupils to produce the four storyboards; each pupil in the group produces one storyboard. This will give us about seven different versions of the exercise.

I will need to set up the groups at the start of the lesson, and explain then that it will probably be necessary for them to complete their one storyboard for homework.

For the last minutes of the lesson, the pupils will be asked to agree in their groups which storyboard they will each produce, using the table on the board as a guideline. We will also agree how these storyboards will be evaluated and presented in a later lesson. I will make clear at this stage how this will link into the next lesson, and will give them a few minutes to say how this lesson has, or has not, contributed to their learning about segmenting text and storyboards.

This is, of course, not a lesson plan, but it does attempt to show some of the thinking involved in planning for learning, and for the acquisition of skills. An important aspect of this lesson is that focus is placed on how to record, present and evaluate, and pupils are helped to see how what they have learned will be applied later. The overall context has been made clear to them.

USING OTHER TEACHERS' LESSONS AS MODELS FOR PLANNING

While you are on teaching placement during your training year, and later during your NQT year, you can learn a great deal from observing experienced teachers within different subject areas of the curriculum working with their classes. Subject areas in which lessons involve the use of equipment are well worth observing, as they demonstrate very clearly a basic planning 'skeleton' which can be useful to you in planning in your subject area.

In terms of helping you with lesson planning through observation, teachers are likely to be prepared to give you their overall objectives for the lesson, though they may not have a formally written lesson plan for it. As an observer, you are in a good position to evaluate some of what is going on in the classroom, and particularly to assess whether the lesson objectives are being met. Discussion with teachers after lessons will help you see how teachers themselves evaluate the effectiveness of their lessons, and will allow you to compare your evaluations with theirs. You will also recognize how experienced teachers manage lessons as a whole, and how they manage interruptions, beginnings and endings.

In terms of using observations as a model for your own planning, a useful exercise is to write what you think the lesson plan would have been if it had been written down, and to discuss this with the teacher afterwards. It is also helpful to plan lessons with teachers, something which you have no doubt experienced as part of your training. If you are offered opportunities for joint planning, it is a good idea to take them.

SUMMARY

In this chapter you are encouraged to think widely about the considerations inherent in planning lessons. In particular you are encouraged to:

- always focus on your intended learning outcomes;
- build in time for pupils to re-engage in your lesson, by helping them recapitulate from the previous lesson, using starters actively for this;
- plan to engage pupils as much as possible in discussion and consideration of the learning and assessment intentions for the lesson;
- set and maintain high expectations, and also cater for all your pupils;
- develop a repertoire of short activities to use when lessons do not go to plan, when lessons are interrupted, or when you get the timing wrong;
- make use of opportunities to plan jointly with teachers or a peer.

STANDARDS

This chapter will help you think about some of the issues implicit in the following standards. Trainees:

3.1.1; set challenging teaching and learning objectives which are relevant to all pupils in their classes. They base these on evidence of their pupils' past and current achievement;

3.1.2; use these teaching and learning objectives to plan lessons, and sequences of learning, showing how they will assess pupils' learning;

3.3.1; have high expectations of pupils;

3.3.3; teach clearly structured lessons or sequences of work which interest and motivate pupils and which make learning objectives clear to pupils;

3.3.4; differentiate teaching to meet the needs of pupils, including the more able and those with special educational needs.

Chapter 11

Running a lesson

This chapter talks you through a lesson, from start to finish, describing each phase of the lesson, summing up the assessment opportunities of each phase, and giving an overall comment for each phase. This approach is intended to gather together much of what has been covered already and allow you to see how it can be applied. Examples of such application are given in relation to a chemistry lesson.

BEFORE THE START OF THE LESSON

Description

1. You arrive early, and as the room is empty you can go in and organize your materials, resources, the board and the seating. When your class arrive, you make sure that most of them are lined up in the corridor before allowing them into the room. Or, you make sure they are all present before letting them into the room. You stand at the door to welcome them; as they go past you into the room, you greet each pupil by name, and if possible take the opportunity to say something personally supportive. You also use this time to explain where you want pupils to sit.

Or

2. You arrive early but have to wait to go in as there is another class in the room; you knew this would be the case, and have organized yourself appropriately, though you know that you will probably have to accept the seating arrangements as they are. You have already decided that for this lesson, pupils may sit in their usual places, but you are also aware that for other lessons you might want to organize them differently. While you wait at the door, your class arrive, in ones and twos, from their previous lesson. You take the opportunity to talk to them in a friendly but serious way, and ensure that they comply with expected corridor behaviour by lining up quietly. When the previous class have left the room, you stand at the door, as above, while your pupils enter.

3 You have planned in advance how you will manage the administrative and organizational aspects of your lesson, including taking the register, dealing with lateness and dealing with lack of homework.

Ongoing assessment at this stage

You make a mental note of the ways in which individual pupils are behaving at the start of the lesson, and use this information to adjust and modify the way in which you address the class, with regard to both tone and language. You quickly notice the pupils' mood, and choose to deploy tactics which will help them contribute positively to the learning atmosphere you wish to create.

Commentary

Your behaviour even before your pupils have come into the classroom indicates to them that you are organized, in control and supportive. You are confident in talking to them in the more informal context of the corridor, and have already set an unspoken agenda in which seriousness of approach, control of the classroom, support for learning, high expectations and commitment to each individual have been communicated to pupils. Your decisions about where pupils are to sit are clearly communicated: these may be arrangements pupils have already experienced; they may be new ones which you organized according to your learning objectives for that lesson; they may be random rearrangements of pupils which you wish to use to break up unsuitable self-chosen groups. You might accomplish this, for example, by giving out different coloured cards to pupils as they enter the room and asking them to sit with all other pupils with the same colour card. This is only a suitable tactic if you have already been able to arrange the room to suit your purposes.

The tendency of pupils not to arrive all together for lessons requires you to plan for how you will manage their entry into the classroom, and what you will do with latecomers. It is advisable not to allow latecomers to interrupt the flow of the lesson; rather, greet them quickly, ask them to sit down, and remember to speak to them at the end of the lesson about their lateness. It is counterproductive to make a big issue of lateness with one individual; you need to consider the effect on the whole class of your disrupting the start of the lesson in this way. It is also worth operating on the basis that if pupils value and enjoy your lessons, they are far less likely to be late.

Schools have homework policies and you should adhere to these policies in order that pupils experience consistency across the school. At the same time, it is worth paying attention to your pupils' personal circumstances; many pupils clearly exist in home circumstances which are not conducive to sitting down quietly after school and doing homework. Find out if your school, or department, runs a homework club, and if so encourage pupils to use it.

Homework can often cause more problems than it is worth, and can inadvertently become the cause of the most inappropriate confrontations and problems. Pupils who fail to do homework are often caught up in the sanctions systems of the school, and required to do detentions, or some other negative kind of punishment which has nothing to do with pupils as learners and everything to do with pupils as transgressors. It is advisable for you to take a long hard look at homework, and realistically weigh up its actual benefits to pupils. It is also advisable to avoid setting a homework on which your next lesson is going to depend; what will you do when half the class have not done it?

When you set homework, ensure that it has a positive learning purpose, such as finding something out, doing a small bit of research in a library or on the Internet, or maybe interviewing people outside school about something pupils are working on. It is also possible to set up long-term homework, such as recording specific events in a diary or journal, or keeping a learning journal, which you check on at specified times when you take the opportunity to discuss with pupils on an individual basis what they have written.

If you are teaching a class of pupils who you can trust to do the homework you have set, you will need to have planned in advance how you are going to respond to what they have done. With such a class, and indeed with all pupils, discussing with them what kind of homework would be appropriate as a way of developing or rounding off their learning from a particular lesson will emphasize not only your seriousness of purpose, but the commitment you have to engaging them in their learning. You will be giving them the opportunity to consider how the intended homework can help them progress.

If the homework is to form the basis of a lesson, or at least provide contributions to a lesson, then pupils need to have been fully informed beforehand. For example, if you set a homework in which pupils prepare some kind of presentation, then you need to have organized in advance how the presentations will take place, so that pupils can complete their homework knowing the context in which it will be presented; in other words, they know its purpose, audience and organization.

Once pupils reach Key Stage 4 and A level it is usually necessary to set homework because of time constraints within lessons. The same principles should apply: in other words, pupils must understand and agree with the purpose and outcome of the homework, and know what will happen to it in your lesson.

All the foregoing demonstrate that homework needs to be set and responded to along these lines:

- it must have a clear and agreed purpose and outcome;
- it must have clear learning objectives;

- it must be set up properly, not in a hurried way as an afterthought at the end of the lesson;
- it can, therefore, if desired, be set at the start of a lesson, when pupils can see that it forms part of a greater whole, and can also grasp its serious purpose in relation to what they are doing;
- its completion requires some kind of acknowledgement (marking of work is discussed elsewhere).

If your quick *assessment* of your pupils' mood tells you that they are somewhat volatile, and need to be calmed down, you should use some or all of the following:

- you talk quietly to individual pupils who seem particularly excited, aggressive, unhappy, asking them whether they are ready for your lesson, and asking if you can help them. You ask them to explain if they can what has caused the problem, and give them a few minutes in which to think things through;
- you notice a small group of pupils coming into the room with their own other concerns uppermost in their minds; they have possibly been involved in an argument or worse during break. You quietly offer them the chance to sort out their grievances among themselves, on the understanding that in five minutes they will put these to one side, and engage properly in the rest of the lesson;
- you sense that the whole class is clearly not ready for the kind of lesson you had planned. You need to change their mood. An effective method is to explain what you are going to ask them to do, and why, and then ask them to put their heads down on their desks and shut their eyes. You talk very quietly to them while they do this, silently indicating to individuals who look up that they need to put their heads down. To produce deeper relaxation, you quietly ask pupils to breathe in and out slowly, maybe while you count to four or five: 'Breathe in: one, two, three, four, five; hold your breath: one, two; breathe out: one, two, three, four, five.' You repeat this several times. After five minutes or so, you quietly ask pupils to open their eyes and sit up;
- an alternative method, once pupils have their heads down and their eyes shut, is to ask them to listen for: first, all the sounds they can

hear outside the room; second, all the sounds they can hear in the room (some pupils will take this as a cue to make silly noises, so you might decide not to use this bit); third, the sounds they themselves are making with their breathing and heartbeat. This method gives pupils something outside themselves and their thoughts to focus on, and helps them relax;

- another heads down method is to talk them into imagining a peaceful place, where they can relax. You might actually talk them into such a place which you make up as you go along.

These methods will obviously only work if you believe in them, and apply them with total confidence. Their value is in helping pupils relax and refocus, which many pupils clearly need a lot of help with a lot of the time. The five minutes or so that these methods take is well worth balancing against the likely difficult lesson you would have without using them. Working *with* pupils' moods and helping them out of inappropriate attitudes is far more productive than confronting pupils, ordering them about and telling them off, and producing even more aggression. Methods such as these (you will no doubt be able to think of others) also convey to pupils that you will always be quietly in control, rather than losing your temper and shouting because you cannot manage the class.

SETTLING DOWN BEFORE THE START OF THE LESSON

1. Pupils have sat themselves where you requested, with some talking.
2. You remind them to remove coats, put chewing gum in the bin, take out what they need from their bags, and put their bags on the floor.
3. Pupils can see what you have already written on the board, which may include learning objectives, the date and a key title or set of words.
4. You have decided that you will use taking the register as a way of establishing a tight start to the business of the lesson, or:
5. You have decided not to waste time on the register at this most important time as you wish to engage the pupils as quickly as possible in the lesson.

6. Possibly, as described above, you have used a calming down exercise.

Ongoing assessment at this stage

You glance round the room continuously to gauge pupils' readiness to comply with these routine instructions. Where you notice pupils lagging behind in sorting out their belongings, you encourage them and also respond quickly and without fuss to pupils who say they have lost their pen, or their book, giving them substitutes, and making a mental note to talk to them about this at the end of the lesson.

Commentary

Once pupils are used to the idea of being asked to sit in different places in the classroom, they will usually do this without a fuss. However, it is advisable to ensure that they know why you are using these arrangements, so you should give them your reasons, either as new ones, or reminding them of past ones. These might be:

- 'I'd like you all to sit with a different person for today's lesson so that you can share new ideas and learn from each other.'
- To an individual: 'I'd like you to sit with X today, because you have both got some interesting ideas about this topic and I think between you you can teach the rest of us what you think.'
- 'We are sitting in different groups for this lesson so that we can learn how to work collaboratively with people we don't usually work with.'

For some learning purposes, you might want pupils to sit in a circle. If you can arrange this before the lesson so much the better, but pupils can be taught how to do this themselves, and making this into a game, or even an assessment opportunity, will help them do it more quickly and purposefully. For example, you might say: 'I'm going to assess you while you do this for your ability to work quickly, sensibly, helpfully and quietly', or 'the challenge is to do this in whispers: see how very quiet you can be', and so on. The aim is to find a way to get pupils to collaborate so that the desired lesson can take place as quickly as possible. Pupils can be *trained* to do these tasks in the desired way!

Once pupils are seated as you have required, your reminder about coats, equipment and bags can be made quietly. It is helpful for pupils to be given an opportunity at some point, probably early on in your time with the class, to discuss *why* these rules are necessary, and what can happen to the good order of the classroom, including pupils' and the teacher's safety, if they are not kept.

If you were able to before the lesson, you have written key information on the board already. If you were not able to, you need to have thought out when you will do this. It is not a good idea to do this while pupils are sitting waiting for the actual lesson to start. Similarly, taking the register may not be the best way of starting the lesson. It is fairly boring for the pupils, particularly in big classes, and can often be a time when they lose focus. It is better to take the register when pupils are engaged in an activity; you can then do it either silently, by visually checking who is present, or by calling out names quietly. Sometimes it is necessary to check on pupils absent from your lesson by asking their friends about them.

Taking the register at the start of the lesson can be used as a way of starting off the lesson in a businesslike way, but it can also cause unnecessary friction, particularly if it is used as a way of silencing your pupils, who then start talking again immediately after you have finished. You have to silence them again, and may produce an atmosphere in the room which you did not intend. It also gives you the challenge of another transition to manage; you have to move from one mode of interaction to another very quickly, which may mean, for example, that within the space of two or three minutes you have to move on from being highly controlling to being highly enabling. Such a small and seemingly trivial action as taking a register sends out a lot of unexamined messages, which you might reflect on.

FIRST ACTIVITY OF THE LESSON

1. You engage pupils in the start of the lesson by a variety of means:
   - a starter;
   - questioning;
   - an introduction by you.
2. You make explicit links between the start of the lesson and the main aims of the lesson.
3. You ensure that all pupils are clear about the aims of the lesson.

Ongoing assessment at this stage

This is the first opportunity to assess the ways in which pupils are engaging in the real business of the lesson. You notice pupils who are having difficulty in engaging, and make a note to pair them up with a different pupil next lesson. You notice pupils who appear not to be listening, or understanding.

Commentary

For most subject areas, teachers are expected to come up with a beginning activity called a starter. Of course, before the National Strategy decided to push this practice under this particular label, teachers already did starters, but by another name. However, focus on starters has resulted in some new thinking about how lessons can be given an energetic and engaging start and has strongly focused on how they can help bring about learning. Some of the available ideas and suggestions are worth using, but it is not a good idea to simply use books with titles like 'Your 100 Best Starters' and expect them to do your job for you. It is advisable to know precisely what your starter is supposed to do for pupils' learning, and how you are going to exploit the learning it brings about in the rest of your lesson. In other words, the starter must be linked to the rest of the lesson. In planning starters, you should consider the main part of your lesson, and then extrapolate from it a key set of learning which a starter could help bring about.

Using a chemistry lesson as an example, if your lesson is going to be about what happens when some metallic elements are heated in air, your starter should have some connection with the learning outcomes you are aiming for. It could, for example, remind pupils of what you hope they already know about metallic elements, by asking them to select from a random list of substances the ones they recognize as being metallic elements. Or, you might pair them to come up with their best guess of what might happen when a metallic element is heated in air, giving them a list of metals to work with; they can write their guesses on post-it notes, which can be put on the wall for all to see and be used as a means of comparison with what they find out in the rest of the lesson. Or you might decide to get them thinking about the connection between heating and burning, by asking them what they know already about what happens when a range of substances, including some metallic elements, are heated to burning point, and what is left when the heat is removed. Their ideas here can also be noted on post-it notes and put on the wall for comparison with the actual outcomes at the end of the lesson. What you are aiming for with these starters is to engage pupils in some initial thinking about the conceptual content of your lesson.

You may decide that *questioning* will be the first activity of your lesson, in which case you should make yourself familiar with a range of questioning techniques, and know how to categorize and vary the questions you will be using. It appears that at least 70 per cent of questions asked by teachers are 'knowledge' questions, such as 'What is a metallic element?', 'What did we learn last lesson?', 'How do we say "What is your name?" in German?', 'Who invaded England in 1066?', 'What is a drowned river valley called?', and so on. These questions do have their place, but you need to move pupils on into questions that stimulate more exploratory kinds of thinking, rather than simple recall.

To continue with the example from a chemistry lesson: the teacher's overall aim is for pupils to understand something about the changes that occur when some metallic elements are heated to high temperatures, and to understand what happens to bring these changes about. A starter to this lesson, therefore, which uses *questioning*, can ask pupils to *speculate* on the basis of what they already know: 'Before we look at some metallic elements being heated, what do you guess will happen to them?' Or, questioning can use *knowledge* recall ('What do we mean by metallic elements?', 'What do we understand a metal to be? Can you give some examples?', 'What do we understand an element to be? Can you give some examples?'), where pupils come to the front to write their ideas on the board, which are then openly discussed by the class. The teacher's approach at this point should *not* be judgemental: the concern is not whether pupils have got the answers right or wrong, but with the level of their thinking and understanding at this stage of the lesson.

Good questioning techniques do the following:

- open up pupils' thinking by avoiding closed questions;
- give pupils thinking time before expecting an answer;
- encourage pupils to respond to each other's ideas and answers, non-judgementally;
- move on pupils' thinking and understanding by altering the kind of question asked, from simpler recall questions to questions requiring evaluation and synthesis.

Ideally, pupils' ideas will be noted on the board or on a flipchart, particularly the final decision the class comes to before the main part of the lesson. In the context of this chemistry lesson, by the end of the starter, pupils might agree on a definition of metallic elements, and might have some agreed guesses about what will happen when some of them are heated. These ideas can then be evaluated after pupils have seen what actually happens.

An *introduction* you choose to give in any subject area might take the form of a video clip, or other visual stimulus, where the pupils are mainly passive recipients of the material. This approach does have its merits, but it needs to be remembered that passive receipt of information does not automatically lead to retention, and pupils will still need opportunities to think, question and evaluate.

After the starter activities, which of course can be far more varied than the simple examples given here, it is important to get pupils to tease out the links between your stated learning objectives (on the board) and what they have just done. At this stage it is also good practice to encourage pupils to ask their own questions about the lesson, and to ensure that those who are still unsure are encouraged to say so. This gives you an opportunity to have pupils helping each other, and even teaching the rest of the class from the front of the room.

With regard to the ongoing *assessment* which you have been doing, which may have shown you pupils who are still not engaged in spite of all you have done, you need to do something to help them before you move the class on to the main part of the lesson. It is not good practice to move on with a lesson while some pupils have still not understood what the lesson is about. There is a variety of methods, some of them derived from the Assessment for Learning materials. Their effectiveness depends on your having established a learning atmosphere in your classroom in which not only is it all right not to understand at once, but pupils are positively encouraged to insist on being helped to understand. You could try one of these:

- ask pupils to show whether they have understood. Pair up those who have with those who have not. Ask the pupils who have not understood to explain what they *do understand*. Ask the pupils who have understood to explain the rest. Ask each pair to produce a quick statement, which the original pupil who did not understand now explains to the rest of the class. You can only ask a few pairs to do this, otherwise you will spend a lot of unprofitable time on this exercise;
- ask pupils who have understood to come to the front and explain, including using the board. Encourage those who have not to ask them questions;
- ask those who have not understood to (possibly) come to the front and explain what they have found difficult. Encourage them to feel confident to say that your explanations were not clear. Encourage them to suggest how you might have made things clearer;
- ask all pupils to consider how they would explain this part of the lesson to someone who did not understand it. Listen to their ideas.

TRANSITION TO THE SECOND/MAIN ACTIVITY OF THE LESSON

1. You make a quick *transition* to the next activity, which is likely to constitute the main business of the lesson. You have organized this efficiently in advance and linked it explicitly with the starter in your planning, with appropriate materials, resources and requirements about methods of working. You ensure, by questioning and discussion, that pupils know the *purpose* of the activity.
2. If the activity involves pupils moving seats, you ensure that they do so quickly and with minimum fuss.
3. You make clear how the next activity will be done: in pairs, in groups or as a whole class.
4. You ensure that pupils have all the necessary equipment to undertake this activity.
5. You give the pupils a *time limit* if this is appropriate, and make clear what will happen when it is reached.

Ongoing assessment at this stage

You note how well individual pupils move into the next phase of your lesson. You encourage those that lag. You note pupils whom you are probably going to have to speak to individually, depending on the nature of this part of your lesson, as in spite of all you have done they still look puzzled. You note pupils who might be able to help others, and if need be move pupils around to do this.

Commentary

Unless *transitions* are well handled they can be time-wasting, disruptive of the smooth progress of the lesson and can open up 'gaps' which convey a lack of purpose to pupils. The best transitions:

- take what has been learned already, and make deliberate connections between it and the next activity; this should involve pupils in summing up for themselves the important points to take forward;

- show pupils what the next activity is intended to achieve in order to develop their learning; this may involve teaching them a new skill, such as paragraphing, or reminding them of skills they already have;
- show pupils clearly how the next activity is intended to be accomplished and get pupils to regroup themselves quickly and efficiently where needed;
- make clear to pupils the skills they will need to deploy; this will ideally involve pupils in deciding what these will be, which can then be noted on the board.

Transitions need to be planned for carefully; it is not a good idea to simply note in your plan 'then the pupils do such and such'. At the start of your work in classrooms, it is sensible to rehearse what you will say to pupils at each transition, before you embark on the lesson. Observation of other teachers will give you help with this.

The *language* you use in conducting your transitions, and your lessons, is also of key importance. You may already have noticed the words teachers use to signal what they want pupils to do:

'Right, listen to me.'
'Pens down and look this way.'
'OK, have we finished that?'
'You have five minutes left.'
'You must listen to me when I am talking.'
'Right, the next thing I want you to do is. . .'

You are encouraged to consider the kinds of messages which are conveyed by these stock phrases, about the relationship between the teacher and pupils and about the teacher's view of pupils' learning. In the examples given above, the teacher sees herself as unequivocally in command, and expects to be obeyed. This approach might not always be the best one to use, and you do need to further consider it, if for no other reason than its abrasive effect on some pupils.

It is likely to be more productive to use the inclusive 'we', rather than the teacher dominant 'I'; after all, the undertaking you are embarking on with your pupils is ideally one of joint exploration and learning. Using phrases like 'I want you to. . .' conveys to the pupils that you are somehow not engaged in their actual learning, but are rather requiring them to perform certain actions which may or may not make sense to them. It is not uncommon to overhear pupils say to each other 'What have we got to do?' when the teacher thinks s/he has explained already. If pupils don't know, then the activity has not been set up properly. In addition, pupils not knowing 'what to do' are not very engaged in their learning; rather they are going through the motions of an activity which someone else has required of them.

Some transitions have to include the learning of *appropriate skills* in order that the next full activity can be accomplished. In this case, pupils can be asked to suggest what skills they will need for the new task, and should be encouraged to question the teacher until they fully grasp what is needed. To use the chemistry lesson again as an example: in making a transition to the next activity, which is to observe some small samples of metallic elements being heated at the front of the room, the teacher might introduce this by saying:

'Now that we have our guesses on the board about what will happen when we heat these metals, how could we test our theories?'

(Pupils make some suggestions, which show they understand the principle of testing hypotheses by experimentation and demonstration.)

'What could we do to make sure we have made accurate observations of the demonstration?'

(Pupils make suggestions, including making notes.)

'We have some suggestions here to help us, like making notes. Can we think of anything we might have missed out?'

(Pupils can't.)

'Do we think everybody's notes are likely to be reliable? Will everyone see things in the same way? What might we do about that problem?'

(Pupils get the drift, and possibly suggest that they should work in pairs to ensure greater accuracy.)

'We have come up with some ideas about this. You have thought really hard. Now we need to make sure we all know how to make notes. Spend

one minute with your partner talking about how you could make your notes as accurate as possible, and then we'll have a top speed reporting back.'

(Pupils do this, come up with a few ideas. Teacher writes these very quickly on the board, and accepts that pupils know how to make notes in pairs. Or, if pupils clearly do not know, the teacher must spend the necessary time showing pupils how to make notes, possibly by modelling note-making on the board. In order to model working with a partner to make notes, the teacher can bring a pupil to the front of the class, and set up a little scenario in which the pupil tells the teacher what to write, and the teacher writes this on the board, or vice versa.)

'Can we quickly remind ourselves of why these notes are important?'
(Pupils offer suggestions.)

'Can we think of what we will be doing with these notes once we have made them?'
(Pupils offer various suggestions, with the teacher encouraging those who indicate that the notes will be needed to test the pupils' original hypotheses.)

'Any other ideas about why we might need these notes?'
(Pupils suggest that they will be needed for writing about the lesson in a more formal way.)

This might seem to be very time-consuming, and you may regard such a set of interchanges as unnecessary, and cutting into the limited time available for the lesson. However, as your aim is to enable all your pupils to learn from the lesson, this must include not only the conceptual content of the lesson, but the accompanying skills content. Most importantly, going through a little scenario as suggested above helps develop pupils' understanding of learning processes, and engages them in thinking in a more holistic way about what they are doing. Once you have spent some time on processes such as this, you will probably find that less time is needed with each subsequent lesson, as pupils begin to be more confident about looking at their learning from this kind of perspective, and about asking questions. In future lessons you would only need to remind pupils very briefly about the importance and practice of note-taking.

If you intend pupils to work in pairs or groups (see Chapter 7 for more details) you will need to have ensured that they know exactly why they have been asked to work like this, what the benefits are, and what you hope they will learn from each other. You will also need to have ensured that they know *how* to work together in groups.

START OF THE MAIN ACTIVITY

1. The pupils are ready to begin, and know what they are to do; this includes a last-minute check by the teacher, possibly asking a pupil to explain again for everyone's benefit.
2. You tell the pupils what you are going to be doing during this part of the lesson.
3. You describe the activity to the pupils in terms of their need to concentrate.
4. You explain how the activity fits in with the overall learning objectives of the lesson.
5. You explain how the results of the activity will be shared when it is completed, and the kinds of responses which will help develop everyone's understanding and learning.
6. You repeat the time limit (where appropriate) and then ask them to start.

Ongoing assessment at this point

There is not a great deal to assess at this stage, before pupils have actually started the activity, but you will still need to keep an eye on how they are all settling down, and with what degree of concentration and purpose.

Commentary

The kind of main activity implied here may not apply in all subject areas, although it is likely that whatever your subject, you will be planning for a main activity in each of your lessons.

Checking for understanding of the task is essential; asking a pupil to explain again is important, and should be set up so that other pupils feel confident to ask even at this stage. More than one pupil can be involved in this, and you should encourage pupils to come to the front of the room to explain. Or you can have arranged pupils in pairs, so that a more confident pupil works with a less confident pupil and ensures that they understand. The activity should not start until you are certain that all your pupils have understood what it is, why they are doing it, and what it will lead on to.

If you sense a certain unwillingness to start on the part of the pupils, it is a good idea to give them little challenges which will ensure that they will want to focus on the task, especially with pupils who do not automatically settle down and do their best. One tactic is to give a time challenge: 'I am going to time you for five minutes while you continue with your work, to see how much you can do in that time, in silence. At the end of five minutes we'll see where you have got to. Starting now!' Another one is to give pupils built-in 'talk time': five minutes on task, one minute talk time. An even more productive approach is to use stop times to examine how things are going, to ask pupils to describe how they are finding the task, to listen to their comments and suggestions, and to use these to redirect them back to the task. In this way, you are directly involving pupils in thinking about the task in terms of learning, rather than simply as something which you are requiring them to do. It is not conducive to overall learning and development to allow some pupils to routinely fail to bother to understand and listen attentively because they know you will 'come round' and explain to them. This leniency on your part confirms them in their disengagement and does nothing to move them on. It also indicates that the activity has not been set up well enough.

In the kind of lesson suggested here, involving quiet working by pupils, probably writing of some kind, you need to be very clear about your role at this point in the lesson. If you decide to move around the room, your purpose should ideally be to make positive comments about what you see pupils doing, and to maintain your overall view of the whole class. This means not turning your back on the class while you talk to one individual, and also means not spending more than a few minutes with anyone. It is worth thinking further about the purpose of this moving around the room. 'Going round' the room, for less experienced, less confident teachers, can often run almost out of control, with pupils putting up their hands for help or confirmation of what they are doing, until you the teacher are run ragged. Because you are in among the pupils, you have vacated your control position at the front of the room, and pupils are good at exploiting this vacancy. You cannot allow this to happen. If this does look like occurring in a lesson, you need to get all the pupils' attention again, backtrack to the instructions and explanations, and reconfirm their understanding. Ask them to continue with their task, and make clear that you expect them to complete it without further help.

Depending on the nature of this activity, it is possible for you to remain seated at the front of the class and to ask pupils to come out to see you. In this way you retain your overview of the whole room and can also pay better attention to the pupils' problems. You can organize a rota for this kind of teaching, making clear to pupils that they will be seen in turn. Do not waste your energy as a result of not having planned, prepared and set up your activities efficiently.

Giving *time limits* for activities can be important in many lessons, although the implications of these do need to be considered. You need to be careful that you are not taking a kind of piecework approach to what pupils are doing, and that you are not hurrying them through something without giving enough time. However, it is important that you remain in control of the allocation of timings for different activities, and that you have set a suitable *pace* for the lesson. It is not advisable to allow pupils to set the pace, which will inevitably drag, nor to let them force you into giving them more time for the activity.

MAIN ACTIVITY

1. Your main activity may consist of pupils working individually, in pairs or groups without any whole class intervention from you.
2. Your main activity may alternatively consist of the whole class working together, with you substantially controlling pupils' interactions and actions.
3. Staged feedback may be embedded in this activity, enabling pupils to see progression, and giving them a chance to consciously link what they are doing with the aims of the lesson.

Ongoing assessment at this stage

In a lesson where pupils are working without your intervention, you have opportunities to evaluate how well they are completing the task, either by reading some of what they have written, or by listening to what they are saying in discussion. For some formal assessment purposes, such as speaking and listening within GCSE English, this part of the lesson can give you opportunities to assess the performance of individuals within groups against the given criteria, though you are unlikely to complete more than five or six such assessments in any one lesson. It is also possible from time to time to use the relative freedom of manoeuvre afforded by pupils working quietly by themselves to pay more focused attention to individual pupils on a one-to-one basis, when you actively teach them something they have not yet grasped.

In a whole class main activity, you have plenty of opportunities to assess pupils' performance and achievement in the light of your learning objectives, and to assess how well all your preparation has worked. You need to consider whether you will have time or opportunity to record any of these assessments.

Commentary

Obviously, main activities come in many different forms, and for a range of purposes. Mention has been made already of the importance of setting up these activities in such a way that pupils can achieve the intended learning or development which you planned for. If your ongoing assessment indicates to you that some pupils are not managing this, your assessment eye needs to be turned onto yourself, in order to start the process of reflection and reshaping the same lesson for the same learning outcomes at a future date. It is also a good idea to analyse the difficulties pupils are having, and make a mental note of inadequate preparation on your part. This should involve deciding whether their difficulties are conceptual or skills-based, both of which would also indicate some shortcomings with regard to your breaking down the content into steps and to your use of language in an earlier stage of the lesson.

This is a further stage of the lesson where you should talk to pupils about what they are doing in terms of learning, contribution to the final outcome, development of thinking, development of understanding, and a grasp of progress made. What pupils are doing should not be talked about as 'work', even though this can be a useful private shorthand for you. To repeat what has already been said about this, what message would you be conveying to pupils if they kept hearing you say: 'Get on with your work'? What does this mean to you, to the pupils? What connection does this have with the idea of learning?

In the chemistry lesson used as an example, the main activity is pupils observing the demonstration of the metallic element samples being heated to high temperatures. Their preparation for this during the starter means that they know the partner they will be working with, they know how to makes notes, they have made guesses and predictions about what will happen and know that their observations will be compared with these, and they know the general learning aim for the lesson. They will be observing as a whole class, and making notes as pairs.

Such a main activity does require tight organization. The teacher needs to decide in advance whether to stop after each demonstration to allow pupils to make their notes (desirable) or whether to rely on their memories and do all the demonstrations before they write their notes (not so desirable). The teacher needs to decide whether to make the comparisons on a running basis (desirable, in order to keep the pupils' interest high, and to allow the teacher to hear pupils' reactions to what they have just seen) or whether to leave these to the end (also possible, and allowing pupils to take a longer overview). By the end of the activity, it is important that the pupils have:

- observed closely;
- made notes collaboratively;
- compared their findings with their earlier predictions;
- arrived at an agreed set of conclusions;
- understood how to write about the lesson for future reference.

CONSIDERING AND DISCUSSING THE MAIN ACTIVITY – THE PLENARY

1. Where appropriate, you bring the activity to an end at the precise time you said you would. You have kept pupils informed of the time throughout the activity.
2. You ask for initial reactions to the activity.
3. You encourage both the negative and the positive reactions.
4. You ask pupils to evaluate the activity in terms of their deriving any benefit or learning from it.
5. You use a range of methods for feedback, depending on the way you ran the activity.
6. After the feedback, you again ask pupils to evaluate what they think has been achieved.
7. Using pupils' suggestions, you agree on a way of recording what has been done, for future use by pupils (this, of course, depends on the nature of the activity).
8. You also set up assessment opportunities for what pupils have done, including peer assessment and whole class involvement.
9. You make clear links with what pupils will be doing in their next lesson, and engage them in a brief discussion about how the present lesson will contribute to it.

Ongoing assessment at this stage

This point in the lesson presents many different opportunities for both informal and formal assessment.

Commentary

The approach during this part of the lesson is to confirm pupils in their key role in the learning process; that is, they tell you what they have achieved, and you give them structured opportunities for evaluating the main activity. This stage is in many ways the most important part of the lesson, because of the opportunities for review and overview which it gives pupils.

In the chemistry lesson used as an example, pupils at this stage are encouraged to arrive at well-stated overviews, which the teacher notes on the board. Pupils consider and then agree the best one. The teacher makes links with the next lesson by asking the pupils what they think they would need to find out next about metals and elements, and about why what they have found out might be important in the wider world.

Whatever the subject area and main activity, it is important to make space for pupils to consider what they have done/learned/achieved, to think about the wider context in which this activity exists, or could be made to exist, and to think about further applications in later lessons. The development of pupils' understanding that learning is about links, contexts, applications in other circumstances and is developmental is an important part of their growth as autonomous learners. Similarly, it is important to develop their understanding that their learning is dependent on a range of factors, including conceptualization, skills and language, and that they are already showing their capabilities in all these areas.

END OF THE LESSON

1. You ensure that you have at least five minutes before the end of the lesson to bring it to a rounded, considered conclusion.
2. Either you have already set homework, in which case you and the pupils remind yourselves of what it is **or** you have left it until the end of the lesson to set homework, in which case you need at least ten minutes at this stage.
3. You organize an orderly exit from the room by ensuring that all materials and resources are suitably put away, all litter is disposed of, all pupils have their belongings with them and are standing behind their pushed-in chairs.
4. You allow pupils to leave row by row, or table by table, using the same friendly and supportive approach with which you greeted them on entry into the room at the start of the lesson.
5. You stand at the door, and talk quietly and in a friendly way with pupils as they go out.

6. If another class is waiting to come into the room, you quickly pack away your own things and leave on time.

Commentary

Pupils' exit from your classroom is as important as their entry in terms of appropriate behaviour, sense of purpose, expectations and general learning atmosphere. It is part of your professionalism as a teacher to ensure that your pupils are going out into the corridor in good order. Standing at the door allows you to confirm your relationship with pupils and their learning: the message given to pupils by this, especially when you back it up with friendly and supportive comments, and praise for achievement, is that they matter to you, and that you are committed to them and their learning.

SUMMARY

This chapter is self-explanatory.

STANDARDS

This chapter will help you think about the implications of the following standards. Trainees:

1.1;   have high expectations of all pupils;
1.2;   treat pupils consistently with respect and consideration, and are concerned for their development as learners;
1.3;   demonstrate and promote the positive values, attitudes and behaviour that they expect from their pupils;
1.4;   are able to improve own teaching by evaluating it, learning from the effective practice of others and from evidence;
2.1;   have a secure knowledge and understanding of the subject they are trained to teach;
2.7;   know a range of strategies to promote good behaviour and establish a purposeful learning environment;

3.1.1; set challenging teaching and learning objectives which are relevant to all pupils in their classes;

3.1.2; use these teaching and learning objectives to plan lessons, and sequences of lessons, showing how they will assess pupils' learning;

3.1.3; select and prepare resources and plan for their safe and effective organization;

3.2.1; make appropriate use of a range of monitoring and assessment strategies to evaluate pupils' progress towards planned learning objectives;

3.2.2; monitor and assess as they teach, giving immediate and constructive feedback to support pupils as they learn. They involve pupils in reflecting on, evaluating and improving their own performance;

3.3.3; teach clearly structured lessons or sequences of work which interest and motivate pupils and which make learning objectives clear to pupils, employ interactive teaching methods and collaborative group work, and promote active and independent learning that enables pupils to think for themselves and to plan and manage their own learning;

3.3.7; organize and manage teaching and learning time effectively.

Chapter 12

Evaluating lessons and formative and summative assessment

This chapter focuses on what you need to do after each lesson in order to ensure that you can plan appropriately for the next lesson or sequence of lessons. It is important that you assess how far you have taken your pupils' learning in each lesson, and that in focusing on learning you see individual lessons as constituent parts of a whole, rather than as single events. Evaluating your lessons, from a set of perspectives, is a most important part of the process of teaching. Without going through this process, you are unlikely to be able to develop your own thinking and understanding, and are less likely to know how to plan for your pupils' development. At this early stage of your career it is not advisable to depend on quick on-the-spot assessments; it is advisable to spend time making notes about the success or otherwise of each aspect of a lesson, followed by further consideration (which may need to include asking for advice, reading relevant texts or consulting earlier notes) of how to replicate success or avoid failure in the next lesson.

REFLECTING ON THE LESSON AS A WHOLE

At the start of your teaching, you will probably not have found it easy to evaluate your lessons, and may well have made comments such as 'the lesson went well, the pupils did what I asked them, and there were no problems with behaviour'. As a brief description of the lesson from your point of view this may well be fairly accurate, and you might feel quite pleased with yourself for having conducted such a lesson. However, such an evaluation tells you nothing at all about:

- your pupils' learning;
- your pupils' view of the lesson;
- the appropriateness of your materials, content and approach, other than by implication;
- the reasons for the lesson running smoothly;
- how you will develop your pupils' learning during the next lesson;
- whether you would know how to replicate such a lesson in future.

This kind of evaluation also raises the question of what is meant by a lesson going 'well'. Pupils doing what you ask, and there being no problems with behaviour may or may not indicate a genuinely successful lesson. Such a comment is superficial and basically focused on behaviour: the pupils were obedient and well behaved.

A more helpful evaluation would pay some attention to the evidence showing whether or not pupils were learning anything. The kind of evaluation given above suggests that there was little actual teaching, and that pupils were mainly engaged in some form of activity. As they did what the teacher asked, the implication is that they could do it, which raises another question: if they can already do something, what are they learning by doing it again?

You will find it far more useful to your own development to spend time considering the bullet points above and being prepared to go back over the lesson in the kind of detail implied. This will give you opportunities to consider:

- what your learning aims were;
- what your ongoing assessment plans were and whether you applied them;
- whether your materials were appropriate for every pupil;
- how you managed pupils' behaviour;
- your overall running of the lesson, including timing, pace, starts and ends.

EVALUATING YOUR LESSON PLAN IN THE LIGHT OF THE LESSON

After a lesson it is sensible to look back over your lesson plan to decide the extent to which it did not contribute to the success or otherwise of your lesson. In the early stages of your teaching, you should expect this to occur quite frequently, and use it as a positive learning opportunity. One of the most common reasons for lessons not fully realizing even the best lesson plans is time: a lesson plan can look very good on paper, but in the sometimes unpredictable circumstances of classroom life, the time planning which looked so efficient beforehand evaporates into something rather more nebulous and appears to exist in some other dimension.

Some reasons for the difficulties encountered with managing time are:

- inappropriate expectations of what pupils will achieve or complete within given time limits;
- lack of thought about how to keep time limits meaningful, shown by failing to stick to them rigorously;
- insufficiently detailed planning of how the expository, explanatory and exploratory aspects of the lesson will be undertaken, allowing them to overrun;
- falling prey to pupils' subtle takeover of the lesson, which they do by working very slowly if at all, but always appearing to be hard at it when you look at them;
- giving too much time for written tasks and group tasks.

In evaluating your lesson plan, it is worth noting down as soon after the lesson as you can those features of your lesson which at the time you were conscious were not working. They are likely to include a number of moments when you realized things were not positively contributing to the learning you were aiming for, and it is largely from this perspective that you should analyse what went wrong.

USING EVALUATIONS AS POINTERS FOR PLANNING THE NEXT LESSON

The example of a brief evaluation given above would obviously not be any use at all in helping you plan the next lesson. However, your answers to the sets of bullet points above would be of use in helping you establish a new starting point for planning; in other words, you can take each lesson and lesson evaluation as a stage in the overall development you are aiming at for your pupils, so in effect each lesson acts as a baseline for the next.

Your evaluation of how well your pupils learned in one lesson must be the key to planning the next lesson. This evaluation is likely to be based on a range of ongoing assessments which you were making during the lesson, which will have included your impression of how pupils responded generally, how they showed understanding through answering questions and participating in speaking and listening, what you observed of their written work, how they responded during the plenary at the end of the lesson, their behaviour in so far as it indicated engagement, interest and enjoyment, and their desire or otherwise to rush out of the room at the end of the lesson.

Such ongoing assessment is largely impressionistic, and needs to be analysed from a more consciously pedagogic point of view, so that you can develop your understanding of how your actions as teacher have produced pupils' responses and behaviours. Such assessment also needs to be supported by the evidence of pupils' learning shown by their written work, if that was part of the lesson. The most efficient way of assessing pupils' learning in a lesson is through the plenary session at the end; this therefore needs to be planned to allow all your pupils to show what they have learned. A good plenary should allow you to assess the level of understanding of all your pupils, and will give you valuable information for your next lesson.

USING EVALUATIONS TO SEEK HELP

Your ongoing assessment of your lesson and your later evaluation of it may lead you to decide that you need some further advice from other teachers. In this case, it is worth being very specific about what you want to know, but it is also important to remember that you are likely to have had problems in the first place because your lesson was not well enough planned and prepared.

It is always a good idea to ask for advice, and it is also a good idea to categorize it mentally, to ensure that you are aware that some advice will be in the form of 'tips for teachers', some will be more thoughtful, and some will not be appropriate for you at this stage. The best advice will help you focus on learning aims and outcomes, and seek to show you how to plan your lessons to enable these to be met, while also offering you some further advice about behaviour management, particularly for the start and end of lessons.

ASSESSMENT[1]

The assessments you apply during and after your lessons are of key importance in contributing to the overall evaluation of your teaching. The ways in which your pupils have performed in response to a lesson will provide you with valuable information when you plan their next lessons, highlighting for you:

- what pupils have or have not understood and learned conceptually;
- the skills pupils have or have not learned and deployed;
- the behaviours, both appropriate and inappropriate, demonstrated by pupils during your lesson;
- pupils' perceptions of the lesson and of their own learning.

The analysis of this information will tell you a great deal about the successes and failures of your lesson planning and teaching, and the results of it should be used in a conscious way in future teaching.

In the course of your work with a class, you will be involved in both formative and summative assessment procedures, and you should expect to be able to use these to best advantage for your planning and teaching. In all instances, you should ensure that your pupils understand the purpose, method and timing of all assessments *before* they undertake the requisite tasks; preferably, you will discuss your intended assessment methods, giving pupils opportunities to question them in relation to the task. Pupils who are experienced in this kind of discussion are also able to suggest assessment methods themselves.

Formative assessment

Quite a lot has already been said in this book, both explicitly and implicitly, about formative assessment as you might use it both in lessons and afterwards. As the name suggests, this is a means of assessment which contributes as immediately as possible to pupils' progress: it forms and re-forms their learning, and is vital as part of the cycle of learn → do → evaluate/be given feedback/assess → redo/ refine/redraft/try again → relearn/learn more → do and so on. This kind of assessment can be carried out in different ways, and does not always have to be done by the teacher; pupils should also be involved as a matter of course, in peer assessment and group evaluations. Your formative assessment can be done during lessons by verbal feedback, discussion and commentary and after lessons by reading written work and commenting on it. In all cases, your aim should be to provide your pupils with clear pointers for the direction they should be going in, which may be expressed as achievable targets for the next lesson or group of lessons.

As a result of your formative assessment, you should be able to pinpoint features of your lesson planning and teaching which brought about success or failure, and take steps to address these where necessary. You need to consider how your formative assessments will lead to your pupils' continuing learning, and thus how they will also contribute to more formal summative assessment.

Summative assessment

As its name suggests, summative assessment is concerned with summing up pupils' achievements at the end of a fixed period and making judgements about them. Within school, summative assessment is used in a variety of ways: at the end of schemes of work, at the end of each half-term, at the end of the school year and at the beginning of Year 7 to establish baseline information for setting. You will be heavily involved in preparing pupils for regular external summative assessments which are now part of the English education system, testing pupils at 7, 11, 14 and 16.

You are encouraged to use the results of summative assessments to inform your planning and teaching; this is likely to be over a longer term than from single lesson to single lesson, but if you have, for example, decided to use some form of testing to establish where your pupils are, it is advisable to use the results as soon as possible, both to underpin your next lesson, and to give important information to your pupils about their level of achievement so far.

MARKING PUPILS' WORK

Marking has been mentioned already, but it is worth discussing again in the context of this chapter. As a means of evaluating how successful your teaching has been, marking can be a very useful exercise, but there are a number of caveats to be applied;

- pupils who have learned well through oral interactions but who are not confident writers will not necessarily be able to communicate their learning through written work;
- some pupils may not have completed the written task when you take it in for marking, making it difficult for you to assess their level of achievement;
- you need to be very certain of the purposes of your marking, and of the level of feedback you wish it to give to your pupils.

Marking written work may reveal a whole host of problems for your pupils, not all of them connected to the learning objectives you intended. The most common of these are pupils' difficulties in expressing their understanding coherently, articulately and legibly, their lack of commitment to written work because they fail to recognize, or are determined not to recognize, its function, and their lack of commitment because of a fear of failure.

Disentangling all these from the evidence of learning, however poorly expressed, is quite a challenge. You will need to decide how you can teach your pupils the skills they lack, possibly after consultation with other teachers, and, of crucial importance, you will need to rethink your whole approach to written work. In your planning, therefore, you will need to think through very carefully the actual purpose and kind of written work you are planning to set, and apply some rigorous questioning to it:

- What purpose will this writing serve for pupils?
- What purpose will it serve for me?
- How will I set it up to ensure that it tells me, and pupils, what we want to know about our learning?
- How do I propose it should be marked, if at all?
- What purpose will this writing serve within the context of the overall lesson?
- Can I set this writing up so that pupils easily see its importance and engage in it with conviction?

In association with the evaluation of your teaching, marking can perform a useful function, but only if it is done very quickly after the lesson, if it provides informative feedback to pupils about their levels of understanding and learning and their use of language, makes clear to pupils how they can improve, and can also lead supportively into the next lesson. For pupils there is little point in receiving back written work which they completed weeks or even months earlier, which has been superficially responded to with a series of ticks and little else. For you, there is little point in marking pupils' work at a distance in time from the lesson which generated it. This is not a good use of your time and will not support your current lesson planning.

SUMMARY

This chapter offers a lot of advice relating to evaluation and planning of lessons. The key suggestions for you are:

- evaluate lessons carefully using the given bullet points;
- use the results of evaluations as pointers for your next lessons;
- use evaluations to form the basis of planning;
- undertake all assessment with clear purposes;
- inform and talk with pupils about your assessment intentions;
- carefully and critically think through your whole approach to marking.

STANDARDS

This chapter will help you think about issues implicit in the following standards. Trainees:

3.2.1; make appropriate use of a range of monitoring and assessment strategies to evaluate pupils' progress towards planned learning objectives and use this information to improve their planning and teaching;

3.2.2; monitor as they teach, giving immediate and constructive feedback to support pupils as they learn. They involve pupils in reflecting on, evaluating and improving their own performance;

3.2.3; are able to assess pupils' progress accurately using National Curriculum level descriptions, and the requirements of Awarding Bodies;

3.2.6; record pupils' progress and achievements systematically to provide evidence of the range of their work, progress and attainment over time. They use this to help pupils review their own progress and to inform planning.

NOTE

1   See Black, P., Harrison, C., Lee, C., Marshall, B. and William, D. (2003), *Assessment for Learning*. Maidenhead: Open University Press. In Chapter 4 'Putting the ideas into practice', there are extremely useful analyses and suggestions of both formative and summative assessment.

Appendix 1

Pedagogy

'Pedagogy encompasses the performance of teaching together with the theories, beliefs, policies and controversies that inform and shape it.'[1]

'Pedagogy connects the apparently self-contained act of teaching with culture, structure and mechanisms of social control'[2]

This appendix offers a brief discussion of some aspects of pedagogy. You might well be wondering why such attention to pedagogy is relevant to you and your teaching, and be ready to consign the whole thing to the realm of 'theory'. You possibly share the attitude to 'theory' that is common in schools and among teachers, and indeed among several thousand of your predecessors on ITT courses; that is, that it is irrelevant, does not help you 'teach', has no practical value and smacks rather too highly of academia and intellectuals.

THEORY

It is much to be regretted that this is the prevailing attitude. It is a very powerfully anti-intellectual stance, taken as a matter of course by most trainee teachers, and often reinforced in them by the attitudes of teachers they work with on teaching practice, one of whose favourite pieces of advice is: 'You can forget all that theory they teach you at the university; this is the real world of teaching and you need to learn some practical stuff.' There is a strong and long-standing tradition of emphasizing the 'practical', which has its roots in nineteenth-century attitudes to education for the masses, as distinct from education for the elite which was based more explicitly on 'character building'. Charles Dickens[3] provides a barbed observation of the former through the character of Mr Squeers in *Nicholas Nickleby*:

'This is the first class in English, spelling and philosophy, Nickleby,' said Squeers, beckoning Nicholas to stand beside him. 'Now then, where's the first boy?'

'Please, sir, he's cleaning the back parlour window,' said the temporary head of the philosophical class.

'So he is, to be sure,' rejoined Squeers. 'We go upon the practical mode of teaching, Nickleby; the regular education system. C-l-e-a-n, clean, verb active, to make bright, to scour. W-i-n, win, d-e-r, der, winder, a casement. When the boy knows this out of the book, he goes and does it. Where's the second boy?'

'Please, sir, he's weeding the garden,' replied a small voice. 'To be sure,' said Squeers, by no means disconcerted. 'So he is. B-o-t, bot, t-i-n, tin, n-e-y, ney, bottiney, noun substantive, a knowledge of plants. When he has learned that bottiney means a knowledge of plants, he goes and knows 'em. That's our system, Nickleby: what do you think of it?'

'It's a very useful one, at any rate,' answered Nicholas significantly.

While it is clear that Squeers' view of the 'practical mode of teaching' is no longer recognizable in the form applied by him, nevertheless the underlying preference for the practical over the theoretical remains unquestioned and taken for granted. It suggests a profound distrust of the whole discourse of academic enquiry and research, and allows some teachers in schools to invest in a stereotype of their university colleagues, which works against the realization of the potential of fruitful discourse and exchange of ideas and understanding. Given that during the controversies surrounding the framing of the first version of the National Curriculum in the late 1980s, politicians and others with some kind of vested interest in controlling education were given public space in the media to attack the idea of 'theory', and were energetically echoed by the then Chief Inspector for Schools,[4] it is hardly surprising that anti-theory positions continue to be so widely and so strongly held.

In spite of this, you are encouraged here to consider how theory, and in particular the theories of teaching and learning bound up in pedagogy, can contribute significantly to your development as an informed, thoughtful and knowledgeable teacher, who is able to move beyond the 'what works' approach to teaching onto a level of understanding and thought capable of developing your classroom expertise well beyond such a limited view of teaching.

WHAT WORKS

The very real problems with the 'what works' approach are that it does not automatically lead on to any more fundamental understanding of or thinking about *why* certain approaches work, and can often mislead teachers into assuming that because pupils have 'done' something, they have actually learned something from it. Opportunities for valuable pedagogical discussion about the *why* of 'what works' are few and far between for many teachers, leading to a situation where teachers are unable or unwilling to interrogate their practices from a theoretical perspective. This means that much potentially valuable insight is never articulated, and what is meant by 'what works' never carefully examined. What is also not examined is what teachers mean by this phrase. There are many possible interpretations, ranging from 'it works because it keeps the pupils quiet and on task', to 'it works in so far as it develops my pupils' learning'. This continuum of reasons is worth considering further, particularly when you reach the end of a lesson and feel like saying the same thing yourself.

Compared with other education systems,[5] English education is particularly poor in terms of commonly held pedagogic positions based on a theorized and learned understanding of how to teach in order that children learn. There are, of course, plenty of approaches, tips for teachers, and sayings of an aphoristic nature, about how to treat rather than how to teach children: 'spare the rod and spoil the child', which one suspects is an attitude still lurking in the subconscious of some teachers even though they may no longer physically chastise children; 'go in hard at first, so the little so-and-sos know you mean business'; 'don't smile until Christmas' and so on. Interestingly, none of these pieces of so-called 'advice' have anything to offer by way of pedagogy, and are based on the application of crude psychology.

METHODOLOGIES AND PEDAGOGY

An increasing emphasis has been placed on recommended *methodologies* since the introduction of the National Curriculum and the National Strategy, and much of the material produced for schools to support the teaching of different subjects exemplifies notions of 'best practice'. The relatively recent focus on assessment for learning, now promoted as an underpinning methodology by the National Strategy, offers ways for teachers to begin to grasp in a more explicit way the links between what they do when they 'teach' and what is happening in pupils' heads when they are being 'taught'.

A key distinction which is useful to remember here is that a *methodology* is not necessarily a whole *pedagogy*. A methodology implies a 'how to' approach, and tends to focus on the teacher as purveyor of that which is being 'taught'. A methodology might work very well for most of the pupils most of the time, but it is likely that it will be predominantly thought of as something which 'works'. When different methods do not work, it is more likely that teachers will search for another method which does work, rather than interrogate the failed method for why it has not 'worked'.

It is therefore useful to regard a *pedagogy* as providing a teaching and learning overview, based on a theorized understanding of learning and teaching, and also based on a particular set of expectations about learning in relation to young people. A *methodology* can be regarded as exemplifying the ways in which the pedagogy is put into practice. You might find it useful to think further about the methodologies which you observe being practised, and to work out the pedagogy they exemplify.

A careful reading of the Standards for the Award of Qualified Teacher Status (QTS), towards which you are working during your training year, reveals a quite strongly promoted though narrowly conceived pedagogy: the emphasis throughout the document is on *learning* and on the requirement for you to show that you can plan for, teach and assess your pupils' learning, however constrained this is. The document quite clearly recognizes the link between assessment and learning, and the importance of lesson planning which is focused on the development of all pupils. What the document cannot do is offer any suggestions for methodologies which will realize the underlying pedagogy.

SOME PEDAGOGIC APPROACHES

'In every lesson we must both consolidate previous knowledge and teach something new. It's rather like a snowball; repetition, consolidation, new knowledge, repetition, consolidation, new knowledge. But the important thing is the new knowledge. It is through this that children grow, not by staying in the same place.'[6]

The quotation above, from a primary school teacher in Russia, clearly illustrates a pedagogy which is unfamiliar in England. While the pattern of teaching she describes might apply within single lessons, it is not usual here to see it operating from one lesson to another. With the pressure to cover the curriculum, it is common to see pupils lagging behind; and once this has happened in only a few lessons, they never make up lost ground. The underlying approach is often not one of consolidating from lesson to lesson, but of asking what pupils remember from the previous lesson before hurrying on to the new content for the current lesson.

In the same Russian primary school, teachers talked of the 'need to break learning down into small, carefully graded steps. These should steer a careful course between "outpacing development" and maximising children's concentration.' Breaking down a *lesson* into small steps is not an unfamiliar process in English schools, but the skills enabling teachers to break down *learning* are not so widespread. In order to break down learning, the teacher needs to understand the cognitive development inherent in the learning, and know how to go through the recursive processes described in the quotation while focusing on very small steps in the learning process. This is not common practice in secondary education in England. In conjunction with the understanding of how to arrive at a pattern of small learning steps, teachers also need to be clear about the language they will use and teach their pupils. It is not uncommon in England for teachers to make judgements about pupils' ability to understand 'posh' words, and to choose therefore not to use them. This has the result of maintaining pupils' language use at an impoverished level, and of undervaluing and underestimating what pupils are capable of.

CONCLUSION

You will obviously reach your own decisions about whether you wish to pursue and develop theoretical positions about teaching and learning, or whether you will prefer to continue with your current approach. It is worth pointing out that intellectual engagement with theory is more likely to keep you interested and alert as a teacher than a more narrow focus on practicalities. It will also provide a useful basis for further study as part of your continuing professional development.

NOTES

1 Alexander, R. (2000), *Culture and Pedagogy*. Oxford: Blackwell Publishing Ltd, p. 540.
2 Alexander, R. (2000) *op. cit.* Chapter 17 examines culture and pedagogy in detail and is recommended reading.
3 Dickens, C. (1839), *Nicholas Nickleby*. Harmondsworth: Penguin Books 1978.
4 Chris Woodhead. Chief HMI (1992–2000) and therefore also in charge of establishing the operational methods of Ofsted.

5 See Alexander, R. (2002) *op. cit.* The position of pedagogy in England is discussed at length in Chapter 17.

6 Alexander, R. *op. cit.*, p. 309.

Appendix 2

National Curriculum outline requirements

This appendix comprises National Curriculum outline requirements for *Knowledge, skills and understanding* and *Breadth of study*. It is included to enable you to see at a glance what your pupils are required to learn when they are in other subject lessons. Bear in mind, therefore, the sheer amount of knowledge and number of skills which pupils are expected to acquire.

DESIGN AND TECHNOLOGY

Knowledge, skills and understanding

- developing, planning and communicating ideas
- working with tools, equipment, materials and components to produce quality products
- evaluating processes and products
- knowledge and understanding of materials and components
- knowledge and understanding of systems and control
- knowledge and understanding of structures

Breadth of study

Pupils are to be taught the above through three broad areas of design and technology activities.

ENGLISH

The curriculum is divided into three broad areas: Speaking and Listening (EN1), Reading (EN2) and Writing (EN3).

Speaking and Listening

Knowledge, skills and understanding

- speaking
- listening
- group discussion and interaction
- drama
- standard English
- language variation

Breadth of study

Pupils to acquire skills in these areas through a range of activities in different contexts and for different purposes.

Reading

Knowledge, skills and understanding

- understanding texts
- English literary heritage
- texts from different cultures and traditions
- printed and ICT-based information texts
- media and moving image texts
- language structure and variation

Breadth of study

Pupils to acquire the above through the study of a prescribed range of pre- and post-1914 English literature, and non-fiction and non-literary texts.

Writing

Knowledge, skills and understanding

- composition
- planning and drafting
- punctuation
- spelling
- handwriting and presentation
- standard English
- language structure

Breadth of study

Pupils to acquire the above through addressing a wide range of purposes, readers and forms of writing, as prescribed.

GEOGRAPHY

Knowledge, skills and understanding

- geographical enquiry and skills
- knowledge and understanding of places
- knowledge and understanding of patterns and processes
- knowledge and understanding of environmental change and sustainable development

Breadth of study

Pupils to acquire the above through the study of two countries and ten themes.

HISTORY

Knowledge, skills and understanding

- chronological understanding
- knowledge and understanding of events, people and changes in the past
- historical interpretation
- historical enquiry
- organization and communication

Breadth of study

Pupils to acquire the above through three British studies, a European study and two world studies.

MATHEMATICS

Knowledge, skills and understanding

- using and applying number and algebra
- communicating
- reasoning
- numbers and the number system
- powers and roots
- fractions
- decimals
- percentages
- ratio and proportion
- calculations
- mental methods
- written methods
- calculator methods
- solving numerical problems
- equations, formulae and identities
- index notation
- equations
- linear equations

- formulae
- direct proportion
- simultaneous linear equations
- inequalities
- numerical methods
- sequences, functions and graphs
- functions
- gradients

MODERN FOREIGN LANGUAGES

Knowledge, skills and understanding

- acquiring knowledge and understanding of the target language
- developing language skills
- developing language-learning skills
- developing cultural awareness

Breadth of study

Pupils to acquire the above through working on nine groups of language-based activities

PE

Knowledge, skills and understanding

- acquiring and developing skills
- selecting and applying skills, tactics and compositional ideas
- evaluating performance
- knowledge and understanding of fitness and health

Breadth of study

Pupils to acquire the above through four areas of activity including games activities (statutory) and three others from a choice of five, one of which must be dance or gym.

RELIGIOUS EDUCATION

Aims and purposes

Pupils:

- learn to understand and respect different religions, beliefs, values and traditions (including ethical life stances), and understand their influence on individuals, societies, communities and cultures;
- explore issues within, across and between faiths and consider questions of meaning and purpose in life;
- learn about religious and ethical teaching, enabling them to make reasoned and informed judgements on religious and moral issues
- develop their sense of identity and belonging, preparing them for adult life as citizens in a plural society;
- develop skills of enquiry and response in analysis, expression, reflection, evaluation and application, through the use of distinctive language, listening and empathy

Content

- Christianity and the other principal religions represented in Great Britain
- how these religions influence individuals, communities, society and the world
- the nature of belief, religion, philosophy and ethics

Development of these skills

- investigation
- interpretation
- reflection
- empathy
- evaluation
- analysis
- synthesis
- application
- expression

SCIENCE

Knowledge, skills and understanding

- ideas and evidence in science
- investigative skills
- obtaining and presenting evidence
- considering evidence
- evaluating

Breadth of study

Pupils to acquire the above through working on six clusters of activities. They must also be taught to use scientific language, conventions, symbols and equations. They must also be taught the health and safety implications of science work.

Appendix 3

Handwriting

The pragmatic reasons for including this appendix are:

- Pupils' weaknesses in writing by hand negatively affect their whole approach to writing and by extension to lessons.
- Pupils with handwriting weaknesses routinely dismiss what they have produced as 'rubbish' and often there is some degree of truth in this.
- This impacts on their view of themselves as learners, and removes any sense of achievement they might have from what they have written.
- Weak handwriting is inefficient.
- Poor handwriting adversely affects the impression received by external markers of examination papers, and in the worst cases makes papers virtually impossible to mark.

The creative reasons for including this appendix are:

- Handwriting, or calligraphy, is an art form demanding precision and finesse, and therefore higher order motor skills.
- Handwritten artefacts can be a source of pride.

Even though pupils are encouraged to make much more use of ICT in their presentation of written work, handwriting is still the expected mode for tests and examinations.

The expectations for children at Key Stage 1 (age 5–7) within the National Curriculum for English are that they should be taught:

- how to hold a pencil/pen;
- to write from left to right and top to bottom of a page;
- to start and finish letters correctly;
- to form letters of regular size and shape;
- to put regular spaces between letters and words;
- how to form lower and upper case letters;
- how to join letters.

For children at Key Stage 2 (age 7–11), they should be taught to:

- Write legibly in both joined and printed styles with increasing fluency and speed.
- Use different forms of handwriting for different purposes (for example, print for labelling maps or diagrams, a clear neat hand for presented work, a faster script for notes).

In spite of these requirements, there will still be pupils in classes you teach, all the way through the school, who cannot write legibly, or cursively. The practice of teaching handwriting in primary schools varies widely, and as there is no expected 'hand' in the English system, children often develop their own ways of forming letters, without regard for any accepted norm. Much of the practice of putting pen, or pencil, to paper at primary level focuses on children imitating what they see in front of them, rather than on using a specifically taught method for reproducing text.

The beginner writer (in our education system age five or younger compared to age six or seven elsewhere) is faced with a symbolic system which is not difficult to learn by sight, but which does make high cognitive demands on children for the purposes of producing writing themselves. Children have to learn to distinguish between lower and upper case letters, to know when the conventions require them to use either, to know how to form letters legibly, and as they grow older, to learn how to write a cursive, or 'joined-up', script.

There are conventions about the formation of letters, though many secondary pupils appear never to have been taught them. For upper case letters involving straight strokes, the convention is to start at the top of the letter with a down stroke: so H for example, is written as I↓ followed after a small space by another I↓, and the letter is completed with a cross stroke, made from left to right. A is formed in the same way, with the two down strokes starting at the apex of the letter. Upper case letters with straight lines and round strokes, such as B, D and P also start with the down stroke, followed by the round stroke/s. These letters have an additional movement, requiring the down stroke to be followed by an up stroke taking the pen back to the top, before the round stroke is added. Upper case letters composed of round strokes mostly follow the same pattern as their lower case versions: the round stroke is made in an anti-clockwise direction, starting at the top of the letter, as in C, G, O and Q.

For lower case letters, pupils have to learn additional conventions. First of all they have to use the anti-clockwise hand movement for many more letters, such as a, c, d, e, g, o, q. Secondly, they have to learn letters which have a stroke below the line, such as f, g, j, p, q, y. Thirdly, they have to learn that lower case letters conventionally take up half the height of upper case letters, and so pupils have to learn to control their pen strokes appropriately.

The anti-clockwise hand movement required for writing some letters does not come naturally to young children, whose instinct is to make clockwise hand movements. Handwriting programmes used in some schools include the use of repeated patterns of letters, to accustom children to the correct hand movements. You may have used these yourself at primary level. These patterns also help develop children's ability to join their letters together in a cursive script.

At age 11 it is possible that you could help pupils remedy some of their handwriting weaknesses, but this becomes increasingly difficult as pupils get older and more resistant.

Ways of motivating pupils include:

- helping them to learn the correct ways of forming letters so that they can write much faster and more accurately;
- giving them a presentational challenge which requires them to produce neat and accurate work, but with some kind of reward;

- giving them external reasons for improving, such as the need for legibility in examinations;
- giving them intrinsic reasons for improving, such as feeling better about themselves as writers, and being able to take pride in what they have produced.

Appendix 4

Teacher Effectiveness Enhancement Programme

This programme, TEEP for short, is covered in brief in this appendix to give you some supportive research findings on which to base your planning and teaching. TEEP is a programme being taught to teachers in many parts of the country, and you will undoubtedly find it worth your while to attend such training if you are given the opportunity. The findings given below sum up the methodological approaches which have been found to produce enhanced pupil performance; the training programme and associated materials offer practical ways of realizing these methods.

This programme grew out of a Maths Enhancement Project, in which researchers aimed to understand what caused differences in performance of similar pupils in different schools and classrooms. The researchers hypothesized initially that it was teacher behaviour rather than teacher personality which made the difference, and their findings confirmed this.

The team found that the following teaching factors correlated positively with gains in pupil test and examination scores:

- classroom management;
- behaviour management;
- direct instruction;
- review and practice;

- interactive teaching;
- varied teaching;
- classroom climate.

The researchers concluded that the most effective teachers tended to be effective in most of these areas, rather than just one. It is evident from this and other recent research that the teacher is probably the single most important factor affecting student achievement, and the implication of this finding is that more can be done to improve education attainment by improving the effectiveness of teachers than by any other single factor.

Some of the findings from the project were that the most effective teachers:

1. Emphasize teaching and learning as their main classroom goal, creating a businesslike, task-oriented environment. They spend classroom time on academic activities, rather than on socializing, or 'free' time.
2. Deploy effective behaviour management: they spend time with new groups teaching the procedures and protocols of expected behaviour, and are consistent in maintaining the protocols and reminding pupils of them. Pupils are given boundaries and know the consequences of overstepping them.
3. Manage and organize classrooms as effective teaching environments, in which transitions are brief, appropriate resources are available and to hand, and little time is wasted in getting organized. The teacher ensures that the classroom layout is appropriate to the teaching/learning activities, and that the classroom is organized and tidy.
4. Actively teach and supervise, rather than leaving pupils to work on their own for lengths of time. They do not rely on textbooks or published schemes but carry the content personally to the pupils. New knowledge is linked to pupils' prior knowledge, and connected, not taught in isolation.
5. Use a mixture of higher and lower level questions, recognizing that questions should stimulate pupils to think. They use a high proportion of 'process' questions, calling for pupils to explain their answers, methods and opinions. They use appropriate 'wait time'

following a question. They wait for longer than the average 0.7 to 1.4 seconds used by most teachers, especially when asking higher order questions.

6. Create a classroom climate which is 'low stress, high challenge'. The climate is relaxed and supportive for pupils. Pupils are willing to ask and answer questions without fear of 'put downs' from other pupils and they feel safe and valued. They have high expectations of the class, and communicate these expectations unambiguously and consistently. They give pupils regular, constructive, specific feedback on their work, and spend time teaching pupils how to work well collaboratively. They create the climate in which pupils can learn.

This information is based on http://www.cchsonline.co.uk/teep/etb/effectiveteaching.htm. For more details, visit this website.

Index